UPCYCLIST

UPCYCLIST

RECLAIMED AND REMADE FURNITURE, LIGHTING AND INTERIORS

Antonia Edwards

PRESTEL

MUNICH . LONDON . NEW YORK

CONTENTS

INTRODUCTION

Antonia Edwards | www.upcyclist.co.uk

WHAT IS UPCYCLIST?

Upcyclist started in 2011 as a blog reporting on the finest examples of creative reuse. Its aim was to showcase the aesthetic possibilities that can occur when transforming something seemingly worthless into something of value. The website is a growing curated collection of projects that cross over into all spectra of the visual and decorative arts, including furniture, lighting, interior design, fine art, sculpture, architecture, fashion design and jewellery design. The *Upcyclist* school of thought encourages us to re-evaluate overlooked materials, objects and spaces in ways we never thought possible and proves that creative reuse knows no bounds.

UPCYCLIST AND UPCYCLING

The concept of upcycling was popularized by the books *UpCycling* by Gunter Pauli (1999) and *Cradle to Cradle: Remaking the Way We Make Things* by Michael Braungart and William McDonough (2002). The term was used to describe the practice of converting something disposable into something of greater use and value, preventing the waste of potentially useful materials, by utilizing existing ones and lessening the need to use new raw materials. In contrast to recycling, upcycling does not require that the materials be broken down. Instead they are modified, altered, enhanced, combined and transformed into objects of a higher aesthetic or environmental value, either for the same function or a completely new one.

The principles underlying *Upcyclist* go hand in hand with ideas about mindful production and consumption. The chief aim of this book, however, is to draw attention to an aspect of upcycling that is too often overshadowed by its links to thriftiness and environmental concerns: the tenet that intelligent reuse is both an art form in its own right and a technique for creating objects of exceptional beauty.

Upcyclist celebrates makers who work with waste materials out of desire rather than obligation, because they best express an idea or lend something unique to a desired aesthetic. Their approach sits in opposition to quick-fix upcycling which, in spite of any intention to be environmentally friendly, can often lead to low-quality pieces that are likely to end up back in the waste

PREVIOUS SPREAD:
Nic Parnell, hat stand made from waste wood coated in nylon flock.

OPPOSITE:
Carolina Fontoura Alzaga, *CONNECT 28*, 2014, chandelier made from bike chains.

stream. More attention should be given to creative reuse which results in beautiful objects that are considered works of art, surpass trends and become heirloom pieces that people want to keep. As a consequence, they are diverted from landfill for several lifetimes.

REFINING REUSE

Appropriation and modification of everyday objects has continued to be a useful medium for artists and designers ever since Marcel Duchamp signed an upturned urinal in 1917. Blurring the lines between art, design and craft, *Upcyclist* aims to illustrate that something made of junk does not have to be rough, rebellious, anarchic, heavy or shocking. Although some of the works in this book have a sense of fun, eccentricity or naive charm about them, others have a surprisingly delicate and understated quality. The new wave of artists and makers are meeting the challenge of creating works that are fresh, clean-cut and refined despite being generated from something old.

Upcyclist does not restrict itself by defining what upcycling is or isn't. Instead it explores beauty in any kind of remodelling, reconfiguring, restoring, reclaiming, repurposing or appropriating, with the intention of inspiring a design-conscious audience.

ARTISTS, DESIGNERS AND MAKERS IN THIS BOOK

The success of a project that incorporates upcycling often depends on the space for which it is intended. With this in mind, this book shines a spotlight on beautiful reuse created for a range of environments, including furniture, lighting, art objects and installations.

The works featured have been created using a wide range of reclaimed sources. Categorized by their main material, projects range from contemporary rugs made from t-shirts (page 70) to restaurant interiors decorated with old doors (page 24), flooring made from vintage belts (page 94), furniture crafted from redundant boat sails (page 80) and lighting fashioned from weathered plastic found washed up on the beach (page 232).

The book profiles 45 artists, designers and makers that come from a variety of creative backgrounds. Few of them have set out to be upcyclists and to define their creations by their upcycling practices would be to oversimplify their work. Their ability to take waste and turn it into something contemporary, beautiful and exceptional, however, is testament to their unique creativity and skill, as well as their ability to challenge our perception of the material world.

What *Upcyclist* strives to capture are the ways in which reclaimed materials make demands of the imagination. Working within the parameters of reusing something others might consider waste creates a challenge that designers and makers relish. It appeals to their thirst for problem solving, naturally encourages innovation and unleashes previously untapped ideas. These creatives not only shape how we think about the things we buy and throw away, but show us that ideas are sparked by the process of upcycling that may not have manifested through any other means.

THE FUTURE OF REUSE

With a new generation of upcyclists setting the benchmark for beautiful reuse, there is infinite potential yet to be discovered. As reuse techniques become more advanced and refined, these

Stuart Haygarth, *Drop Chandelier*, 2007,
made from plastic water bottles collected
from Stansted Airport security.

practices will expand to appeal not only to the luxury market but the mass market too, as companies begin to investigate upcycling potential on an industrial scale. As resources become scarce, all markets should be considering the life span, reuse value or disposability of every manufactured product from the outset.

As a result of our ongoing love affair with all things vintage, the idea of second-hand being perceived as second-rate has almost dissipated. Upcycling goes one step further, enabling us to create a contemporary style of our time, as opposed to replicating a bygone era.

The evolution of upcycling runs parallel with the times. As new technologies emerge, new species of reusable materials become available. How they will be reused in the future remains to be seen.

WOOD

EL NEBOT DEL PERSIANER

Salvador Nadal Belda | Valencia, Spain

VENETIAN BLINDS > LIGHTING AND FURNITURE

Founded by Salvador Nadal Belda in 2012, El Nebot del Persianer ('nephew of the blinds maker') is a multidisciplinary design atelier focusing on interior design, product design and communication. With a passion for environmentally sound materials, Belda has developed a range of contemporary home products made from old Venetian blinds. The inspiration for the project came from Belda's uncle Lucas Sanz Belda, who had a career in making, hanging and repairing blinds for over 50 years. Belda explains, 'Initially, all blinds were hand-crafted from cane. Years later, they were made redundant as factories began to make shutters from wood. This inspired me to reuse the old blinds for another function. By utilizing these autochthonous materials, the project became a tribute to an object that had become characteristic of Mediterranean towns.'

Born out of a love of craftsmanship and with reference to a historical and cultural context, his contemporary lights made from blinds are designed to combine the traditions of the past with the hope of creating a sustainable future. With the help of Lucas, Belda was able to make the most of first-hand knowledge of how the blinds were originally manufactured in order to upcycle them into something new. 'We use materials that are at our disposal not only for the benefit to the environment, but to create objects with soul,' says Belda. 'They are composed of materials that have surrounded us whilst we were growing up. Giving a second, functional life to an object is a beautiful concept and this is something new objects cannot compete with. Sustainable practice makes the most of materials that have already been used and doesn't rely on using more materials and energy to harness them. The product itself needs to be as environmentally friendly as the manufacturing process, since one without the other is useless. We not only like unique objects, we love the idea of reusing and extending the life of an object that can no longer serve its original function. Since childhood I have always loved objects that tell stories about how people lived long ago. I think we all have a fondness for the things in our daily lives that have been recovered from our roots and are reminiscent of times past.'

OPPOSITE:
Milano circular suspension lamp made of salvaged natural wooden blinds. The shade can also be painted in different colours.

Adela suspended lamp and storage container and Maru work table. The table is made of solid oak coated with natural oils made from plant resins, with a recycled wooden-blind pocket for storing books, magazines and other objects.

Sant Antoni Street in Belda's town of Aielo de Malferit in Valencia. Old blinds are salvaged from the windows and doors of local houses when they need replacing.

Tilu standing lamp, also available as a floor and suspended version. The lamp's graphic aesthetic is designed to create warm indirect light reminiscent of the sun that filters through the blinds during calm, summer, mid-afternoon siestas.

HÖST RESTAURANT

Jonas Bjerre-Poulsen and Kasper Rønn, Norm Architects | Copenhagen, Denmark

RECLAIMED WOOD, WINDOWS AND PALLETS > RESTAURANT INTERIOR

Norm, a design practice in the heart of Copenhagen working in residential architecture, commercial interiors, industrial design, photography, graphics and art direction, was founded in 2008. The Höst restaurant project started with a range of dinnerware designed by Norm for the Danish company Menu in 2012. It was inspired by the eclectic way in which many Danish chefs were beginning to work with New Nordic cuisine in Copenhagen. Seasonal dishes were served on different kinds of materials. Wood, stone, coloured stoneware and textiles were used as a way of symbolizing the element that the produce had come from. The result was a collection of tableware in a colour palette of greys, dirty blues and greens combined with wood and slate.

To launch the dinnerware, Norm came up with the idea of making an urban farmyard restaurant. Jonas Bjerre-Poulsen explains, 'We talked about how good food tastes out in the open, the simple, rural life, a low-key restaurant in the mountains on vacations to southern Europe or eating at a country inn in Denmark. We took all those elements and interpreted them in a contemporary urban context, and tried to create the same atmosphere indoors.'

In collaboration with Danish restaurateur Cofoco, Höst was built using primarily reclaimed materials that they felt had the right patina and authenticity. Tables were designed from old ceiling constructions, wood ceilings crafted from Euro pallets and found windows repurposed from an old hospital. 'Almost every element is custom-made for the place. Even our Mass Light lamps, which we designed for the Danish company &Tradition, were sandblasted to get just the right surface and tone to match the concept. The reused materials were small gifts that gave us new ideas, with all their stories, tactility and sensuality,' says Bjerre-Poulsen.

Inspired by a mix of Japanese aesthetics, American minimalism and Scandinavian simplicity (whereby materials stand out as something beautiful), the treatment of old materials at Höst is in keeping with Bjerre-Poulsen's and Kasper Rønn's overall design philosophy. In fact, the name of their practice, Norm, derives from an interest in working with existing traditions and norms that have been refined through millennia, as opposed to always searching for something new. Bjerre-Poulsen says, 'We want our designs to not only be made of good materials and with good craftsmanship, but to embody beauty and history and, most importantly, outlive fleeting trends.'

OPPOSITE:
A view through some of the rooms in the basement. The floors were vertically integrated to let as much daylight into the old cellars as possible. On the chairs, furs add warmth and provide good acoustics. The door in the background is made from old flooring.

ABOVE:
Wood ceilings throughout are crafted from old Euro pallets dotted with company stamps. The small tables, inspired by simple planter tables, are made from the same material. The small window, sourced from an old hospital, offers a view into the working kitchen. The coat rack in the background is made from old bottle dryers.

OPPOSITE:
View through to the private dining room with simple Shaker-style chairs in varying nuances of grey. Inspired by traditional construction, the table is assembled with big nails to create a rough aesthetic.

ABOVE:

The bar is made from beams salvaged from an old roof construction. Resembling a pile of wood drying in a farmyard, the beams are piled up with small pieces in between to separate them. Old vintage lamps hang from the reclaimed wood ceiling. Raft stools were designed by Norm for the Danish brand &Tradition.

OPPOSITE:

More than 4 metres long, the private dining table in the basement is made from parts of an old roof salvaged from a school just outside Copenhagen. On the wall, old, used chopping boards covered in beautiful patterns from years of cutting are a decorative feature. The lights hanging above the table are old industrial lamps. The table is also set with the New Norm dinnerware that sparked the whole project.

BON RESTAURANT

Corvin Cristian | Bucharest, Romania

Designer Corvin Cristian initially trained as an architect before spending 10 years building sets for the film industry, where his projects ranged from period villages to spaceships for major American and British productions. 'It offered a variety that rarely occurs when creating interior projects in the real world,' says Cristian, whose approach to interior design has been influenced by his experience in film. He says, 'Cinematographers are contemporary magicians: they create illusions stronger than reality sometimes. Working in this field develops one's ability to create memorable experiences, which is useful when designing for the hospitality industry.'

For Bon Restaurant in central Bucharest, the client wanted to create a French bistro that would appeal to a refined clientele. With the aim of creating luxury from waste, Cristian incorporated 200 reclaimed doors, windows and blinds into the interior design. Some of the doors appropriated for the wall panelling were originally used to fence off building sites, which explains their extreme wear and graffiti scrawls. Others had just been thrown out onto the street. 'In this area and Romania in general, there is unfortunately a craze for demolishing old buildings. Our approach to this design was an attempt to keep some memories of the disappearing past alive,' he explains.

Most of the doors were left exactly as they had been found. In some cases the colours were altered to meet the discreet three-tone colour scheme of white, blue and red. Cristian says, 'The moment we decided to run with the idea, the whole team (including the client) began hunting around for any redundant old doors. We were lucky to find so many of them.'

He adds, 'The idea of reusing came naturally to me. I always strive to incorporate authentic elements into my projects and the application of the materials is an organic process. We look for the materials we need but, if something stunning shows up, then we might change part of the project in order to accommodate that specific item. I enjoy saving beautiful items that otherwise might have ended up in the garbage bin. I almost never look for these pieces in antique shops since it wouldn't give me as much satisfaction as finding them on demolition sites or in abandoned areas.'

Only a few new items were added to the interior scheme of the restaurant, such as the Art Deco porcelain pendants, Verner Panton lamps, silver candlesticks and a handful of designer chairs. Cristian explains, 'They get more value by being shown against a backdrop of old unpretentious materials. I think that the high-end feel has more to do with elegance and discretion as opposed to the shine of new and expensive materials. The charm of an old world comes naturally from the proportions and textures of the beautiful doors.'

OPPOSITE CLOCKWISE FROM TOP LEFT:
Bon Restaurant on 33 Strada Smârdan. The restaurant exterior adds the quintessential colours of the South of France to the streets of Bucharest.

Verner Panton lamps add to the restaurant's contemporary feel and provide a contrast with the old doors on the walls.

Some of the doors were originally green and had a Germanic feel, as they were sourced from a town in the west of Romania. These were painted blue to fit the South of France theme.

OVERLEAF:
Doors were used to break up the length of the space and create intimate booths.

Graffiti on the found doors was left untouched. Doors were rescued from a building site where they were being used as a fence around a demolished house. A contrast with the old doors is created by placing the silver candlesticks directly in front of them.

Sections were cut out of the doors to create shelving units used to display wine bottles.

The original found doors that were used to fence off the demolition site.

The wall lights were specially designed for this project. They have thin metal arms covered in copper, with the textile cable and bulb fixtures left visible. The carefully positioned light sources create a theatrical yet cosy atmosphere.

HENDZEL + HUNT

Jan Hendzel and Oscar Hunt | London, United Kingdom

South-London-based Hendzel + Hunt specialize in furniture design using sustainable and reclaimed materials sourced from the streets of SE15. After leaving school, Jan Hendzel spent several years mastering the craft of pattern making in the field of engineering. In order to hone his design skills, he then went to Central Saint Martins to study for a BA in product design. Oscar Hunt has always been interested in simple mechanisms, in particular the ways in which objects are constructed, move and interact with each other. Studying 3D design at Brighton University, he was able to form a deep understanding of material properties and industrial processes. He met Hendzel while working as a cabinetmaker and they opened their studio in 2009.

'When we started out, many people were beginning to make products from reclaimed materials which we felt not only lacked finesse but still referenced their original form in a rough manner,' says Hendzel. 'Our aim was to produce work that honoured the less valued reclaimed materials that were available in abundance. We wanted to reinstate them to a former glory by treating and processing the work with a high level of care, expertise and experimentalism.'

The reclaiming process is complex and time-consuming. Wood is sourced from derelict houses, old buildings, church floors and wooden pallets. For larger projects the team go to specialist wood yards in and around the greater London area and also work with trees that have come down due to subsidence or storms. The former life of the scavenged materials helps to drive the narrative of their work, but also throws up the unexpected in the form of contamination, rot and woodworm, as well as old nails that snag and blunt. Once they have found the wood, it needs to be trans-

ported, inspected for possible contaminants or foreign bodies and then stored. The wood has variable drying times and it can be up to two years before it is ready to be used. Each individual piece must be handled and painstakingly checked before use.

To Hendzel and Hunt, however, these potential drawbacks are attributes that allow them to have a close relationship with the wood they acquire. Hunt says, 'The challenges of our work affect our production on many levels. Making handmade, bespoke products with a limited availability of materials hinders our ability to produce in larger batches. We are forced to combine reclaimed wood with other types of "off the shelf" wood in order to make our business economically viable, but we strive to keep certain principles behind our work: sustainability, localism and craft.'

Traditional techniques are employed alongside CAD software that aids the designers' understanding of balance, proportion and composition. Materials are usually entirely repurposed rather than appropriated. There may be clues that give an indication of the materials' previous life, but the work is essentially made from scratch. 'Reclaimed elements lend depth through narrative, but the skill for us lies in making an entirely original object, not just reusing an old one,' says Hunt.

By producing high-end products and furniture through upcycling waste materials, their work is intended to extend our perception of the limits of reuse and challenge our attitudes towards value. 'Historically the best cabinetmakers created exquisite pieces of furniture from expensive and exotic timber. Although deforestation and climate change have altered our physical world, our desire to own and use beautiful objects remains,' says Hendzel.

OPPOSITE:
High Shore cabinet, a special commission for the London store Folklore. Based on a traditional bureau design, reclaimed materials were used in the production of all components. A feature of the cabinet is the hinges which, in addition to the locks, were designed in-house.

ABOVE:

Detail of the Hendzel + Hunt studio.

OPPOSITE:

Hinckley table from the Made in Peckham range. The legs of the table are made of six pieces of wood that are interlocked in a unique formation and locked together with two large dowels. The tabletop is made from discarded wooden pallets. Pictured with Kirkwood chairs made from reclaimed hardwood and Victorian floorboards.

Love seats made from laminated plywood with dovetail joints. The hand-carved seats and backrests are made from reclaimed timbers. This specially commissioned pair of love seats are inspired by the traditional tête-à-tête, and are designed to keep lovers entwined. Couples have the option of sitting side by side or in a nesting position. The love seats can also be positioned with the chairs conjoined end to end, so lovers sit face to face.

ABOVE:
The first collection of Gowlett stools was made entirely from discarded wooden pallets found outside the studio's perimeter. This newer version is made with reclaimed oak, black walnut and teak.

OPPOSITE:
This 12-foot-long banquet table was designed especially for The Shop at Bluebird, Chelsea. The form of a tree is seamlessly integrated into the table and appears to grow from its centre.

ABICI
ACNE
ALEXANDER WANG
ANNINA VOGEL
ANYA HINDMARCH
APC
AQUASCUTUM
BELSTAFF
BASSIKE
BLOCH
BURBERRY
CHARLES ANASTASE
CIRE TRUDON
COMME DES GARCONS
CUTLER AND GROSS
DEMY LEE
DKNY
D.L. & CO
EARNEST SEWN
ELIZABETH AND JAMES
EMMA COOK
ERDEM
ERICKSON BEAMON
GARY GRAHAM
GENESIS PUBLICATIONS
GLOBE - TROTTER
HARI
HARTFORD
HEIDI KLEIN
HELMUT LANG
HERVE LEGER
ISABEL MARANT
J BRAND
JAMES PERSE
JASMINE DI MILO
JOHN DERIAN
JOHN RICHMOND
KITSUNE
KRIS VAN ASSCHE
KRISTINA T
LACOSTE
LARA BOHINC
LIBERTY OF LONDON

LINDA FARROW
LUELLA
LULU FROST
MAJE
MARC JACOBS
MAISON MARTIN MARGIELA
MALIN + GOETZ
MELISSA ODABASH
MULBERRY
NDC
NUDIE
NILI LOTAN
NYMPHENBURG
ORLEBAR BROWN
ODD MOLLY
OLE HENRIKSEN
OPENING CEREMONY
OSSIE CLARK
PAUL SMITH
PETER JENSEN
PETER HARRINGTON (ANTIQUARIAN BOO
RAF SIMONS
RICHARD NICOLL
RIKA★
ROZAE NICHOLS
ROGUES GALLERY
RUPERT SANDERSON
SARAH ARNETT
SEE BY CHLOE
SONIA BY SONIA
SPLENDID
STEVEN ALAN
THOM BROWNE
THOMAS WYLDE
TOM BINNS
TOYWATCH
TRETORN
TSE & TSE
VANESSA BRUNO
VANS
JOHN VARVATOS
VIVIENNE WESTWOOD
WILLOW

Brivido
bianco

BLEU NATURE

Frank Lefebvre | Roubaix, France

DRIFTWOOD > LIGHTING AND FURNITURE

Frank Lefebvre's vision for driftwood began in 1995. As artistic director of Bleu Nature, he has now created a catalogue of around 300 lighting and furniture designs that breathe new life into a raw material moulded by water and time. All the driftwood at Bleu Nature is collected by hand from beaches and shores around the world. Although each design is unique, all have the potential to be reproduced. In collaboration with a reclamation affiliate, around 150 tons of wood have already been selected and transferred to the Bleu Nature workshops.

Lefebvre frequently refers to Henry David Thoreau's book *Walden* when describing his job, a book often referenced for its libertarian and environmentalist ideals. 'I wholeheartedly agree with Thoreau's desire to return to nature and this was a big part of the inspiration behind Bleu Nature. Like the Japanese writer Tanizaki in his work *In Praise of Shadows*, I am not attracted to shiny surfaces but rather those which tarnish over time. I have always admired driftwood, which allows you to see the passage of time on matter through natural erosion. My designs illustrate time transcribed into form and object,' says Lefebvre.

Starting out, Lefebvre's initial challenge was working out how to design with such a unique material. 'This is always a challenge for my assistants, especially when they are new to the company,' he says. 'The solution is to love driftwood and choose it with atten-

tion and care, classifying by size, shape and colour. Mother Earth is very good at giving us the same shapes, the same kind of wood, long and straight, short and twisted, big and winding. When you have understood the soul of driftwood perfectly, it becomes very easy to create a good finished object every time and also reproduce the original design.'

He adds, 'We have to reuse our waste. We have no choice. Our planet is a finite area, with limited resources, but I have always tried to explain through my creations that we need to mix raw and wild materials with technically advanced processes.' At Bleu Nature, driftwood is combined with other materials such as resin, leather, wool, stainless steel or transparent acrylic glass, which creates the appearance of driftwood travelling through water. Designs are created to suit a range of interior styles, always with the intention of making an impact.

'Driftwood is a medium and a part of my story. I used to say that designers are like sponges. They absorb what they see in the world around them and recreate it through their art. The only originality is in their eyes and in their personal history. This is what we call spirit. I'm a man of my time who realized he had to do something for the planet and it turns out that driftwood doesn't harm Mother Earth. It's recycling that is simply beautiful.'

OPPOSITE:
Occasional tables from the Pop Fluo collection.

ABOVE:

Collected driftwood.

Artistic director of Bleu Nature Frank Lefebvre
with his team.

OPPOSITE:

Josephine Fizzy chandelier made from driftwood,
acrylic glass and chrome steel. Pieces of driftwood
are surrounded by bubbles in acrylic glass, creating
the sense of a moving stream stopped in its tracks.

ABOVE:
Nilleq and Kisimi side tables, made from driftwood
trunks and branches and acrylic glass, resemble a
slice of a river frozen in time.

OPPOSITE:
Louise Crusoe wingback chair made from
driftwood and old planks with a leather or
fabric seat.

LES M&MDESIGNERS

Martin Lévêque and Mathieu Maingourd | Brussels, Belgium, and Nantes, France

WOODEN PALLETS > FURNITURE

Martin Lévêque and Mathieu Maingourd met at design school in Troyes, France, in 1999. Before creating Les M&Mdesigners, both had gained experience designing for the luxury market. Maingourd worked as a designer at Céline in Paris creating luxury eyewear and jewellery. In 2006 Lévêque embarked on a furniture and design collaboration with designer Xavier Lust.

Inspired by designers such as Gaetano Pesce, the Campana Brothers, Enzo Mari and Droog, Lévêque and Maingourd have a multidisciplinary approach to design. Social and environmental concerns are combined with an aesthetic simplicity and a philosophy that the limits of design can offer them a play area. Upcycling was something they had developed in their early days of design school, but their interest in the practice evolved further after they travelled to developing countries where they saw the many ways in which people are forced to be creative with the few resources they have.

Lévêque says, 'As upcyclists we work with recovery centres and associations, waste-collection sites and flea markets. We also get materials from companies and friends or simply find them on the street. With the wooden pallet projects, we selected the pieces that were the best fit for our concept and allowed us to tell a story before finding the simplest, clearest method of production.'

With issues such as rust, fragility, repair and renovation, reusing reclaimed materials doesn't come without its difficulties, but Lévêque and Maingourd have discovered many benefits. 'Reclaimed materials allow us to decrease production costs and make clever and conscious short cuts, such as reusing things that have been made using technical processes. Producing a plastic piece for a one-off project from scratch, for example, would be difficult and expensive and would have a negative impact on the environment. We like the idea of giving a second life to unwanted objects and putting them on the stage. It's interesting, fun and clever to use these objects in a different context. Materials distressed by time and their life cycle are also an expression of our culture,' he adds.

In addition to their interest in creative reuse, Lévêque and Maingourd are advocates of open-source production. In 2013 Lévêque created the collective *Libre Objet*, a website where designers submit instructions on how others can recreate their designs using the Free Art License. Maingourd explains, 'It is good to diffuse the process of production by allowing people to access DIY processes, as it lessens the impact on the environment. Upcycling and reuse are active movements in times of capitalist crisis but, beyond this, it is a fun and creative way to design. We support a system of production that shows a critically different positioning of thought in an ageing consumer world.'

OPPOSITE:
Charles Edouard armchair made from double-faced pallets. Inspired by the famous LC2 armchair by Le Corbusier.

Cinchas deckchair made from double-faced pallets.
Cinchas is Spanish for 'straps'.

OPPOSITE:

Charlotte Up shelving made from double-faced
pallets, inspired by the work of French architect and
designer Charlotte Perriand.

WINDOW HOUSE

Nick Olson and Lilah Horwitz | West Virginia, United States

RECLAIMED WINDOWS AND WOOD > SUMMER HOUSE

The idea for the Window House was something artists Nick Olson and Lilah Horwitz had talked about on one of their first dates. 'It was really just a silly drawing on a scrap of paper,' says Horwitz. 'We romanticized the idea of building something with a whole wall of windows that would allow you to stargaze or watch sunsets from the inside. Having started as a lovers' whisper, circumstances seemed to make the stars align and we just went for it. It was a risk, but we are both young and thought it would be prime time to do things that might not be completely practical! One of the big inspirations behind the project was the book *Shelter* by Lloyd Khan. It has fallen apart at the seams from so much love.'

Olson and Horwitz both have a passion for making. After studying fine art in New York, Horwitz creates one-of-a-kind, handmade garments that she describes as 'the love child of art and journalism'. Rather than creating seasonal collections, she makes site-specific pieces inspired by her immediate surroundings. Describing herself as a nomad, she learns about each new environment through the act of making. Olson is a photographer who practises contemporary collodion photography; he is also a baker, woodworker and log builder. The couple both work as artists and use the cabin as a holiday retreat in between jobs and projects.

Situated at the edge of a forest in the hills of southern West Virginia, the majority of the lumber, hardware and even roofing of the Window House was reclaimed from an old barn on the property. A lot of time was spent disassembling the structure piece by piece, with great care taken over saving and stacking the lumber, even to the point of straightening the nails. The windows were collected during a road trip the couple took through Pennsylvania, stopping at yard sales, antique stores, salvage yards and any place that looked as though it might have an old window lying around. Each window has its own story. The first was found in a vacant barn, another was found in the old farmhouse built by Olson's great-grandfather and a third from a salvage yard under the Brooklyn-Queens Expressway in New York City.

Putting the 18 × 12 foot wall of windows together was like solving a jigsaw puzzle: there were only so many formations that allowed them to combine many rectangles into one big rectangle. 'When we started, we didn't have an exact layout design for the windows. The process was very organic, choosing a window, measuring it, placing it for the best composition and then putting it up,' explains Olson.

As well as their drive to cut down the demand for new building materials, Olson and Horwitz were drawn to using reclaimed materials because of their availability, cost and aesthetic qualities. The total spend on the project was just $500. Horwitz says, 'There is no way we could ever have afforded a house with an entire wall of glass if we were buying a new giant window. Being creative with reclaimed windows gave us the opportunity to achieve a big wall of light, as well a great view.'

A sawyer originally owned the property that stood where the house now stands. He had built the old barn from lumber milled from trees on the property. Olson says, 'It was an incredible history we were working with. To be able to employ those materials in a new way on the same land was such a wonderful experience. It's a house with many generations of stories built into it. It was important to us to learn how to build a living space that connects us to the land, rather than separating us from it.'

OPPOSITE:
The old pod stove, which was donated by a friend, sits upon rocks found at the treeline on the property. Garments by Lilah Horwitz.

ABOVE:

The house sits right at the edge of a forest and overlooks breathtaking views of the mountainous landscape. Since building it, Olson and Horwitz have been dreaming up plans for many new projects, all geared towards sustainability. They also hope to build similar places that will be available for public interaction.

OPPOSITE:

The structure is a hybrid, part shed and part post-and-beam construction. The exterior wood was left raw and the interior planed and sanded to various degrees.

The house aglow with candles and kerosene lamps by night.

OPPOSITE:
Horwitz with her dog Barley.

ABOVE:
The couple wanted the house to capture the
changing light throughout the course of the day.
Pictured here on a warm afternoon, the sun covers
the interior with patterns of orange light.

NIC PARNELL

London, United Kingdom

After graduating in toy design and interactive play from Brighton University in 2009, Nic Parnell decided he wanted to do something more physical than simply trying to get his ideas to market. He stumbled across Hendzel + Hunt, who were renowned for their flair for design and specialism in reclaimed furniture. After working as their primary maker for two years, learning about joinery and cabinetmaking, his interest quickly shifted from carpentry to contemporary surface finishing. He began to collect dead wood from the forest, fuelled by an interest in its form rather than its grain or rarity. After experimenting with the wood, his initial designs led to a few commissions for installations and events. He then successfully released his own line of products at the London Design Festival before setting up his own company.

Much of Parnell's work explores the contemporary processes that manipulate the surface and structure of wood, giving new value to otherwise forgotten or unwanted sources of timber. His Arbor lamps from the Outside In collection are made from dead branches picked up from the forest floor and covered in luxury surface finishes. These include nylon flocking, bronze and even high-gloss piano finish lacquer, all of which create fresh and compelling aesthetic qualities.

Enlisting the help of friends who work in forestry clearance and coppice wood maintenance just outside London, Parnell is able to source wood locally, legally and ethically. He also works with tree surgeons to source branches that would otherwise be shredded, and salvages sheet wood and sawn timber from construction sites and private house refurbishments. 'I realized I was just as interested in making as I was in designing but didn't feel comfortable contributing to the demand for new goods made from new materials. As well as reclaiming old materials, there is a lot of potential in repurposing objects. This can be a great starting point for new concepts. The re-appropriation of industrial components or manufactured objects is another way to avoid waste,' he says.

He adds, 'In the majority of cases, the form of the original wood plays a large part in the development of my ideas. My work fulfils a desire to repel geometry and engage with nature for its intrinsic qualities. Every object carries its own characteristics, which I highlight or mutate to create a contrast with the materials I decide to work with. I continually play and experiment with surface finishes and details. The materials I use are limitless.'

For Parnell, working with reclaimed materials provides him with the freedom to create and experiment outside the realms of traditional design processes. 'When upcycling, a key element of the final outcome is already provided; it is then up to the designer to re-render or recompose the reclaimed elements into something new with flair and inventiveness. The challenge of reworking existing forms is always new and refreshing and I'm happy when I can avoid repetition,' he says.

OPPOSITE:

Outside In: Arbor table lamp in turquoise nylon flock finish. Once the bark is stripped back and sanded, nylon fibres are electrostatically charged to polarized, sprayed glue. The process produces a texture that is soft to the touch, similar to velour upholstery. The electric cables of the lamps are wired through the branches so that they are hidden from sight.

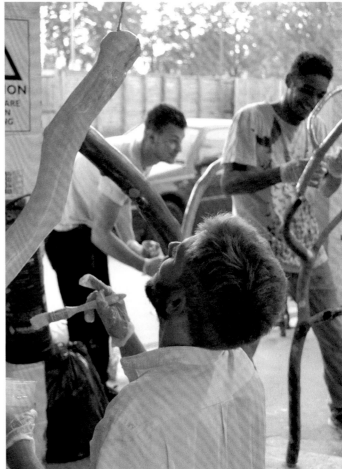

ABOVE:

Wood waste on the forest floor of private woodland in Northiam, East Sussex. For Parnell, scouring the woodland floor is sometimes the best part of the job. The wood requires penetrative treatment to resist mould and wood-boring insects. It can take three or four months before it is ready to be used.

Arbor lamps in progress. Parnell and his team prime branches with an epoxy resin to add rigidity before they are coated in nylon flock.

OPPOSITE:

Hat stand in nylon flock finish. This tree-like form was built Frankenstein's-monster-style from sycamore offcuts felled by London-based tree surgeons. New branch shoots are carved and sculpted to mimic the true divisions of the branch. To allow the branches to be modular, they are cut above the division and rejoined with hardwood dowels and pins to lock them into place (see also pages 6–7).

Outside In: Arbor table lamp in black nylon
flock finish.

Outside In: Mars Bark Arbor table lamp. The
otherworldly, cratered surface comprises graphite,
aluminium and an acrylic-based resin binder.

TOP:

La Noir Arbor table lamp. This special-edition lamp
is made from wood that was found in a bog, rotten
to the core. Once it had been dried and treated for
fungus and wood-inhabiting insects, the wood was
resinated to fossilize its features. Layers of epoxy
resin were then applied to thicken and amplify
its relief texture. It was finally sprayed using a
polyurethane high-gloss piano finish lacquer.

BOTTOM:

Arbor floor lamp in electric-blue nylon flock finish.
The fibrous surface absorbs more than 90 per cent of
light, producing a striking pop of colour.

MARKUS FRIEDRICH STAAB

Frankfurt am Main, Germany

Markus Friedrich Staab has been working as a visual artist since 1986 and has exhibited his work internationally. Since 2010 he has been working with recycled materials and found objects. 'I am particularly interested in giving value and meaning to something that has been overlooked, to free the object from its traditional use and turn it into something special,' he says. 'Through this process, furniture that was once used on an everyday basis becomes a self-sufficient work of art. It is an exploration of how traditional and historical objects can gain value by a mere change of perspective. I am particularly fascinated by these themes of furniture as sculpture and art as objects of utility.'

Staab transforms each piece of furniture into a one-of-a-kind object. Chairs that were once mass-produced and homogenous are not just recycled and refurbished but become singular and unique. Most of the works are made from furniture that people have thrown away or that he finds in the streets. He also buys from various sellers at flea markets and dealers. 'These objects have a present, zeitgeist feeling; they tell stories that can only be told by something that has been used on a day-to-day basis,' he explains.

Rather than applying paint to the entire table or chair, in many of his works Staab lets the natural beauty of the wood shine through. Using spray paint, colour is added to the feet of a table or a flash of fluorescent green is applied to a seemingly insignificant part of a chair. His artistic approach is influenced by German minimalism, particularly the abstract painter and sculptor Rupprecht Geiger. The colour palette is inspired by the Danish artist Poul Gernes and the work of Josef Albers. Staab says, 'Albers inspired me to not do too much.'

He adds, 'I use the imperfection of the found material to show the beauty of mortality. The colours I use, especially the neon, bring modernity to the chair. It is the love for the daily things that we surround ourselves with, their unique shape and expression, which gives me hope that all is not lost to pure consumerism.'

OPPOSITE:
Crown Yellow and Grey, 2012. This Russian kitchen chair was found out on the street. The broken backrest was removed and the seat engraved before being painted and lacquered with 12 layers of boat varnish.

OPPOSITE:

Berühmter Deutscher Maler, 2013. Translated as
'famous German painter', this old garden chair has
been painted with neon and lacquered 12 times.
After the furniture is spraypainted with graffiti
colours, each piece is given up to 15 layers of 2K
lacquer to preserve the imperfections in the wood and
create a high-gloss finish.

Orange Lipstick, 2011. The seat of this 1960s chair,
donated by a friend, was remade from three planks
found in the playground that Staab takes his
children to.

ABOVE:

From the *Gang of Spiders* series, 2013. Mid-century
chairs were bought from a convention centre near
Cologne. They were cut to look out of shape, coloured
with spray paint and lacquered 12 times.

TEXTILES

BOKJA DESIGN

Hoda Baroudi and Maria Hibri | Beirut, Lebanon

RECYCLED JUTE, RICE BAGS, COFFEE BAGS AND CANVAS > FURNITURE AND INSTALLATION

Bokja Design, named after a precious piece of fabric used to wrap a woman's most treasured possessions, is the brainchild of Hoda Baroudi and Maria Hibri. Located in the Quartier des Arts of Saifi Village, Beirut, Bokja is a design and craft studio making one-off furniture and installation pieces using a mix of old and new materials. The studio's unique aesthetic reflects pride in the past, celebrates the overlooked and tells stories that resonate with the contemporary world.

Although she originally came from a journalism background, Hibri has always had a passion for collecting antique furniture. She used to source pieces from around the world and haul them back to Lebanon, where she would sell them. Baroudi was an economist but, after travelling to Central Asia, she developed a rich collection and passion for diverse textiles. The two met at a furniture fair where Hibri was exhibiting and in 2000, Bokja Design was born.

In a city where local crafts and trades are becoming fewer and fewer, Bokja strives to preserve tradition by working with local artisans. 'It is the city of Beirut that sets our stitches in motion,' says Baroudi. 'Our assemblages are a celebration of the differences that bring us all together in the most unexpected ways. Bokja became our way of re-imagining different possibilities and creating new legacies from ideas that were once overlooked.'

Resourcefulness is a large part of Bokja's ethos. No piece of fabric ever gets wasted. This leads to cross-pollination in their work as a leftover piece from one design finds its way into another. 'Using tactile experiments, we have created a visual vocabulary through the way we combine disparate materials and ideas,' Baroudi explains.

The backdrops for most of Bokja's assemblages are made from humble materials such as locally recycled rice and coffee bags, jute and canvas. These are upcycled into precious material through artisanal embroidery, hand-painted imagery and fabric manipulation. 'The dichotomy of these humble materials being elevated through such intimate and hand-crafted details creates an interesting combination visually as well as conceptually,' says Hibri.

She adds, 'As designers, we are drawn to the charm of the way things used to be, when people cherished time, embraced luxury and had a personal investment in their possessions. These objects carried with them legacies that were passed on through generations and transcended time. We strive to recreate this emotional attachment by preserving the past. It's about injecting new life into things that have been left behind. The creative process is as free and exploratory as possible, with no limitations on where it will lead. We always work from an idea rather than towards one. Responding to the materials allows us to be more intuitive and natural in the way we work.'

OPPOSITE:

And Then There Were None, 2013, Cuadro Fine Art Gallery, Dubai, UAE. In this installation, each tactile sphere represents a different political leader throughout history. In parallel with the nursery rhyme 'Ten Little Indians', the work explores the timeless phenomena of dictatorship, playfully questioning a day when there will be none.

Nymphéas and Aría soft tables. Nymphéas is named after Claude Monet's water lily paintings. The upholstery contains recycled jute, hand-painted fabrics and embroidery.

We Are Tyred, 2012. For this street installation
in Beirut, Bokja upholstered motorcycle tyres
in textiles. Traditionally burned in street riots to
voice the public's ongoing fatigue and frustration,
the textiles pacify any political message whilst
maintaining poetic symbolism.

Embroidery in progress for a pouf called Roam Free.

This Desert Rose armchair from the Migration
Stories collection demonstrates Bokja's signature
assemblage style in beige and white with hand-
embroidered birds. The collection is about packing
up your belongings and becoming displaced in
search of a new beginning. It depicts borders as
disappearing bleached walls and possessions as
bundles of hopes and dreams.

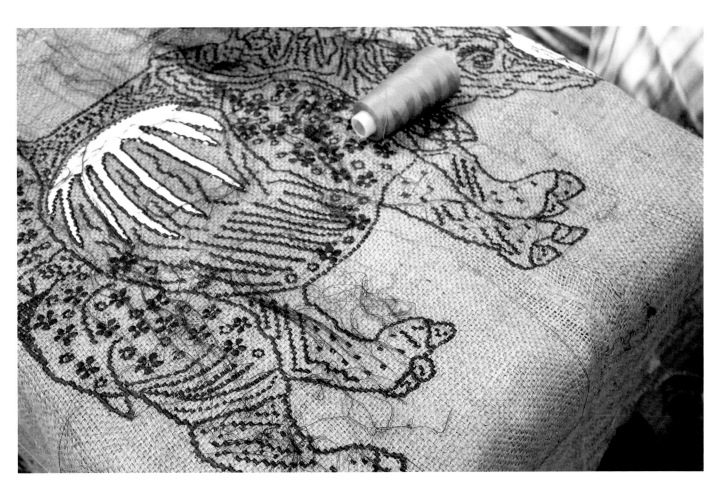

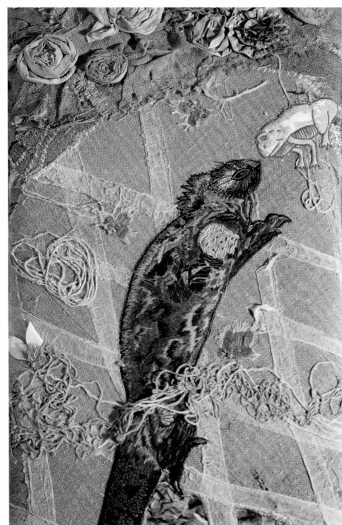

Local crafts and trades in the city are decreasing.
Bokja strives to preserve them by collaborating with
a family of artisans who work from a dilapidated old
Lebanese palace. Everything is made by hand with
meticulous attention and love of detail. Combining
artisans, carpenters and designers, there are at least
14 hands behind every design.

STUDIO BRIEDITIS & EVANS

Katarina Brieditis and Katarina Evans | Stockholm, Sweden

T-SHIRTS, WOOLLEN SWEATERS, TEXTILES > RAG RUGS

'All material is good material, if only you find the right use for it' is the mantra of Stockholm-based textile designers Katarina Brieditis and Katarina Evans, who have been sharing their curiosity about textile techniques since 2001. Brieditis has worked as a freelance designer since 1996, creating products for companies such as Linum, IKEA, Gudrun Sjödén and Rörstrand. Evans is an embroidery specialist and teacher also involved in the conservation of antique textiles. Sharing a mutual interest in recycling fabrics, they have worked on a number of collaborative projects, including Re Rag Rug, an ongoing experimental design project that started in August 2012.

For a 12-month period, Brieditis and Evans set themselves the challenge of designing one unique rag rug per month using textile waste, with each rug made using a different technique. From Stockholm's Salvation Army donation centre, they retrieved t-shirts and sweaters that had shrunk in the wash or were too ripped, stained and worn to be resold or donated to charity. Employing a variety of methods including sewing, plaiting, crocheting, knitting, macramé, rolling, cutting, appliqué and embroidery, they also experimented with scale, relief effects, three-dimensionality and dyeing processes, all in the name of giving the rag rug a brand new face. The goal of Re Rag Rug was to find interesting techniques suitable for unique handmade pieces as well as for sustainable industrial production, giving value to material that would otherwise be considered worthless.

Starting with the material, the design process worked in reverse. 'The challenge of working with limited colours and materials inspired us to create interesting expressions with a high artistic value,' says Evans.

Reproducing an idea using this method, however, was one of the biggest challenges they were faced with, particularly when it came to achieving colour continuity. 'Shade differences can completely kill the overall design,' says Brieditis. 'There is a constant refining of each design at each stage of product development to find potential ways of working with discarded textiles on a larger scale,' Evans explains. 'We wanted to see if it was possible to achieve continuous production of rugs using waste and recycled materials. It was about working out which differences in design we would have to accept and whether there are advantages in compromising when a unique piece is reproduced. Is it at all possible to accept variations in design and quality when working with materials that are always changing?'

The rugs resulted in a travelling exhibition starting at Landskrona Museum, Sweden. Evans and Brieditis continue to find production solutions for each of the 12 designs. The Kasuri and Squeeze rugs made from excess waste from t-shirts are already being produced by women in India. The rug Re Orient is also being reproduced out of waste from Stockholm's Myrorna recycling centre in collaboration with RemakeBolaget, a craft studio that engages with the long-term unemployed.

'Many of the rugs are made with craft techniques that do not require large spaces or machines and could therefore be manufactured by cottage industries in textile-producing countries. Using waste is ecologically sustainable while also being socially sustainable, as the production becomes a platform for developing crafts and creating work,' says Brieditis. 'Man has always sourced materials from the close, natural environment. In the urban lifestyle of today we have mountains of waste. Using it should be second nature.'

Katarina Brieditis at a t-shirt fabric excess market in India. The rug Kasuri is produced in India, where t-shirt waste is generated. The makers are Indian women who are given the opportunity to work from home.

Old t-shirts cut into rags for the crocheted rug Re Orient.

ABOVE:
ABOVE:

The original Kasuri rug and a reproduced version made from t-shirt factory excess. The rugs are woven with a braiding technique. Kasuri is a Japanese rug made from woven fibres that are dyed to create patterns in the fabric.

OPPOSITE CLOCKWISE:

Woollen selvedges from a weaving factory in Latvia. Waste clothing is also sourced from the Salvation Army in Myrorna and from swap shops.

Detail of Aquarelle rug made from patchwork discarded woollen sweaters. The Kantha stitches are inspired by embroidery techniques seen in India, Pakistan, Bangladesh and Japan. The rug also employs a colour-blocking technique whereby each patch has its own composition made from sweaters in similar colour tones.

Detail of Re Orient, an oriental-style rug made of crocheted rags from discarded t-shirt material in red-orange tones. The rug is a symbiosis of the Swedish kilim and a crocheted granny blanket. The idea was to give value to a technique usually considered kitsch or low in status.

Brieditis making wall-to-wall Confetti carpet from woollen sweaters. The rug is made from lots of tiny cut triangles, some of which were waste from the first rug in the series, Tailor. The pattern is designed to resemble a marble floor.

Rosengång, meaning 'rose path', is a new take on the traditional
Rosengång Swedish weaving technique that has a decorative
rose-like border. Made from sweaters, the rug is a winding path
that creates the sensation of walking on soft moss.

OPPOSITE:
Tailor is so-called because of its resemblance to suit fabric.
Made from black and grey woollen sweaters, the pattern is
formed from folded diagonal stripes that look like an enlarged
twill or herringbone weave.

YELI GU

Shanghai, China

FOUND FURNITURE > INSTALLATION

Yeli Gu graduated from Donghua University with a BA in graphic design. Now an award-winning stylist, designer, art director and multimedia artist, Gu first made her mark with global campaigns for clients such as Nike, Coca-Cola, Wieden + Kennedy and Nokia. In addition to her interest in everyday objects, a preoccupation with her native Shanghai is apparent in the variety of media she works with. One of her projects, *Wool+*, is a collection of seating made from abandoned and damaged chairs found in Shanghai's alleys or *nongtang*. Juxtaposing the old with the new, she used visual wit to bring these relics of Shanghai's past into the 21st century with fun, brightly coloured fabrics and woollen pompoms.

Paying homage to the deprivation of post-war China, the textiles used on the chairs reference the resourcefulness of a generation of men and women who developed special weaving techniques to fix broken furniture. 'They would create something beautiful without even realizing it,' says Gu. Having lived in a traditional *nongtang* herself, she was inspired by the strong sense of community and the ways in which unwanted items would be left in common areas for people to use, blurring the boundaries between public and private space. She says, 'Shanghai is a vast, sprawling city going through fast change. Every day it can seem different. So much history is being discarded in the rush for progress. I wanted to show that

even amongst the detritus of everyday life there can still be beauty. These objects can be found almost anywhere in Shanghai if you look hard enough.'

As part of the project, she created a moving installation whereby the chairs were driven around the city on rickshaws. Chairs were parked up on the side of the street so that the reactions of passers-by could be filmed. The chairs caused a sense of delight and an inclination to touch the soft fabric. 'It placed artists in conversation with non-artists and the urban environment, forming an interplay between logic and absurdity, reality and imagination, rationality and existentialism, traditional culture versus the culture of consumption, socialism and capitalism,' says Gu.

Gu's way of working is to experiment with different ideas and techniques until she finds something that sticks. For *Wool+*, she wanted to show that beauty can be found and recreated in everyday discarded objects. 'I could have reproductions made in China, but the objects would have no patina, no soul. I like that the objects have previous lives and stories. Most of us need less than we have, yet we all want more. As long as our desires remain the same there will be no real change in our consumer habits, but there is a glimmer of hope. Lots of small changes in what we decide to buy and throw away can make a big difference.'

OPPOSITE:

Wool+ Chair, 2011, made from a found carved wood chair. Woollen pompoms bring a sense of humour and fun to the chairs whilst also symbolizing the juxtaposition of young and old generations.

OPPOSITE:

Wool+ Bench, 2010, and *Wool+ Chair*, 2011, made
from found furniture and wool. In Shanghai's
alleyways, furniture is frequently found left in
communal areas or out on the street. This creates a
space for communities to sit and socialize, blurring
the boundaries between public and private space.

ABOVE:

Wool+, 2010. Gu created a moving exhibition by
displaying her furniture pieces on rickshaws that
were driven around the city.

DVELAS

Enrique Kahle | Pamplona, Spain

RECOVERED BOAT SAILS > FURNITURE

Enrique Kahle studied architecture at the University of Navarra. He now co-runs the practice Kahle & Arauzo Arquitectura in Pamplona, northern Spain. Kahle and his team work on a diverse range of projects spanning from urban planning and large-scale residential builds to bespoke pieces for interiors. In 2009 he set up DVELAS, a collection of furniture and accessories made from redundant boat sails. The name of the collection is a play on the phrase *de velas*, meaning 'of sails' in Spanish.

Sails are collected from ports, sail makers and individuals, mainly from Hondarribia, La Coruña and Barcelona in Spain as well as La Rochelle in France. For Kahle, the initial motivation for reusing this material was obvious. 'With use, ship sails deteriorate, which makes them useless for exact navigation. However, the materials still have excellent qualities and there is currently no channel for recycling them – something so beautiful would simply be thrown away. All we needed to do was come up with design solutions,' he explains.

A key concept behind DVELAS is that the beauty of the materials must be intrinsic to the designs. Inspired by the poetry of the sea, Kahle merges his architectural influences with observation of sailing techniques, navigation and nautical construction. 'We want the material to work in a dignified manner and create designs specifically to add value to the sails so that they continue working as they did in their previous life and maintain their story. The fabric is not used as a lining or as decorative upholstery but rather to hold up the loads.'

An example of this can be seen in the lounger and easy chair Barlovento-Sotavento, whose name means 'windward-leeward 'or 'downwind and upwind'. The design is inspired by the heel of a sailing boat and the ways in which the boat is counterweighted by the crew when they sit on one side. It also takes inspiration from the different courses and winds that require different sail positions to navigate.

The used sails arrive in varying conditions and once the material is selected, Kahle and his team work out the best way it can be applied. Each sail is used to create a limited series and each piece is tagged with the origins of the sail, the manufacturer and the boat it belonged to, as well as its base port. Using the same zigzag sewing techniques and patterns that are employed by the sail maker when making sails from scratch, any numbers, logos or plastic parts found at the seams are often incorporated into the design. This not only makes each piece unique but reuses the character and handiwork of the original sail maker. 'The charm of the sails partly comes from their beautiful patina. New sails don't carry the same emotional value as a material that has been exposed to the seas,' Kahle says.

OPPOSITE:
Trimmer, named after the crew member responsible for adjusting the sails. The chair has three supports made from bent iron or inox tube, recovered sails and rope. The sail fabric is adapted to the chair with the help of the tension of the ropes.

ABOVE:

Collected sails at Pasai Donibane in Pasajes de San Juan, Gipuzkoa, Basque Country, Spain.

OPPOSITE:

Génois Cheslón loungers made from recovered sail fabric, lacing ropes and metal eyelet holes and filled with expanded polystyrene pearls. This is a comfortable waterproof couch that adapts to the shape of the body. In sailing, genoa is the name given to the large triangular jib that overlaps the main sail and is often used in regatta cruises.

The Barlovento-Sotavento or 'windward-leeward' lounger and easy chair draw inspiration from the different sail positions required to navigate. Made from aluminium and sail fabric, the design permits dual use depending on how it is positioned.

MEB RURE

Istanbul, Turkey

SARI SILK REMNANTS > UPHOLSTERY

Meb Rure graduated in industrial design from Middle East Technical University in 2010 before settling in Istanbul, where she now heads her own design studio. Although she mainly works in industrial design, her work also crosses over into spatial design and art installation. Rure's recycled silk chair, ottoman and stool is a family of furniture made from handcrafted American white oak and waste silk remnants that occur in the making of traditional saris.

It was the vibrant colours of the material that inspired Rure to make the furniture collection, as well as the opportunity to provide work for unemployed women in Nepal. She says, 'My objectives were to create an efficient product and to use the material in a beautiful and effective way.'

The project posed a design challenge because Rure needed to find an innovative way of using material piecemeal to upholster a chair. Remnants from textile factory waste were assembled into a skein by Nepalese women. This was then used to cover handmade sponge balls one by one, which together form a comfortable upholstered seat for the furniture. The inspiration for the colourful design came from a range of ideas. Rure says, 'I had lots of eclectic images in my head: 1970s hippy clothing, gypsies gathered in a corn field, Mongolian shepherd families with all their colourful equipment and belongings. The ethnic-inspired blend of colours felt warm and natural, a lot like the material itself.'

Rure is a firm believer in letting the material lead the design process and that the more problems there are to solve, the more interesting the end result. She says, 'Reclaimed materials force designers to find unusual solutions. Upcycling is the reincarnation of the material. In creative hands, the way we shape waste materials can get better and better. This is exemplified in experimental products and small-scale production. With the rise in environmental awareness, we will see everyone start to think about how they can reclaim waste, not just designers.'

OPPOSITE:
Recycled silk stool. The ethnic-inspired colour scheme is designed to bring a fun and cheerful quality to an interior space. All the colours in the remnants come from natural dyeing processes.

Sponge balls are covered in colourful waste textile
ribbons sourced from Nepal. The most difficult aspect of
using recycled ribbon is that scissored textiles can tassel,
so the fringes are hidden during the wrapping process.

Recycled silk chair and ottoman. Colour combinations are chosen to create a rainbow effect and a sense of uniformity across the collection. American white oak legs are designed to be easily assembled and disassembled to aid transportation and decrease the carbon footprint.

BRUT CAKE

Nicole Teng | Shanghai, China

FOUND FURNITURE AND VINTAGE TEXTILES > UPHOLSTERY

Taiwan-born Nicole Teng studied in Taipei before moving to Shanghai in 2007. After university, she worked in the advertising industry for 10 years. As her work took her around the globe, she became more and more inspired to fulfil her dream of becoming an artist. Teng's creative concept Brut Cake was presented in 2011 and she opened her shop in Shanghai the same year. In contrast to industrial design, Brut Cake devotes itself to handcrafted, useful and functional art objects made from redundant pieces. Teng collects old materials and objects such as furniture parts, drawer handles, broken strollers, school tables and even barbershop chairs, some of which she keeps in storage, ready to be adapted into her work. She also reupholsters her reclaimed furniture with antique textiles. To capture the raw and original elements of her products, the name 'Brut' references the primitive style of the Art Brut movement that originated from France. The word 'Cake' evokes the notion of life's simple pleasures.

In 2007 the economy in Shanghai was rising and the city was growing rapidly. Teng says, 'You could see lots of big construction in the city, high-rise buildings, luxury boutiques and car showrooms were opening. The city was peeling off its old skin to make way for renovations and new construction. Shanghai had previously experienced an era of occupation by European countries. This meant that many Western buildings, Art-Deco style furniture and homeware had been injected into the city. Many Shanghai people were desperate to get rid of "old time stuff", which meant that a lot of beautiful old furniture and fabrics were being abandoned. I had always been very interested in old and used objects. To me, those things had their own spirit. I started to collect, repair and reuse them with my own ideas.'

Teng takes her inspiration from a lifestyle once found in the old town of Shanghai. During the rise of communism, the government took away private property from the rich. Houses were divided into several parts and assigned to different families who lived in tiny spaces, in some cases just one room that served as a multifunctional living space. Most living necessities were repaired and recycled many times to make sure they would last for a long time. 'Those people were the most creative,' says Teng. When Brut Cake was first presented in 2011, however, she had mixed reviews. 'Chinese people couldn't understand the value in my work. For them, the materials reminded them of poor, difficult times. Now, the situation has changed. New, modern things have replaced the old too quickly and some people find my work makes them nostalgic about the simple life.'

The characters depicted in Teng's reupholstered furniture are created through the arrangement of patchwork textiles. 'It's about revealing the faces of the chairs, sofas and stools,' she says. Teng also believes the old Chinese handwoven cotton fabrics she uses have their own spirit. After cutting the fabric, she composes the images before handing it to tailor Xiao Ji for sewing.

Teng's furniture was not initially an eco brand but, after earning media attention, she came to realize the importance of the idea. She says, 'China has become a world factory where countless products are produced and exported to other countries. You can't help wondering how soon we will use up all the available resources. There are also many skilled craftsmen who can't survive because their skills can't compete with the efficiency of the factory machine. I believe people will see the value of upcycling as these resources become increasingly scarce and expensive, even in China.'

OPPOSITE:
The Judge, 2013. Teng created the face of a fox on what was originally a judge's chair, used in court.

ABOVE:

The fabrics Teng uses to upholster her chairs were originally discovered at an antiques market. She then spent two years trying to find the origin of the fabrics: a village on a small island close to Shanghai. They are strong and organic, made with indigo dye. As they are antique and no longer being produced, Teng works hard to not waste any of the material. In addition to Art Brut, her designs are influenced by the roughness and visual impact of Expressionist and Aboriginal art.

OPPOSITE:

Chairs, sofas, stools and benches are collected from second-hand furniture sellers. Teng also buys more delicate pieces from antique dealers, most of which are broken and need repairing. She works with craftsman Mr Huang who, since retiring, is able to continue using his lifelong skills at making, upholstering and repairing furniture.

ABOVE:

Coaster Sofa, 2011. The design for the chair derived from a series of small recycled fabric pieces Teng was using to make coasters before one day deciding to join them all together.

OPPOSITE:

King and Queen of Monster Kingdom, 2010. After finding two old chairs with high, straight backs, Teng chose to depict a king and queen to match their regal feel. The images are inspired by a Paul Klee painting.

Antique Rocking Pony, 2013.

TING LONDON

Inghua Ting | London, United Kingdom, and Los Angeles, United States

LEATHER BELTS > FLOORING AND WALL PANELLING

After graduating from the Royal College of Art, Inghua Ting set up her London design studio in 2000 and a second office in Los Angeles nine years later. Ting's design ethos centres around the reuse of old and new materials to create luxury products. Her tiling for walls and floors celebrates the history and patina of vintage leather belts that have been worn for decades and as a result carry a unique aesthetic that is virtually impossible to replicate. Ting also makes a collection of handbags, wallets and home accessories made from mis-dyed or overrun car seatbelts as well as reclaimed silk vintage ties.

'The inconsistency of the belts we source dictates a variation in the execution of every bag, wallet or tile we make. Leather in particular has a very distinctive wear pattern and it is not something that can be easily faked. The narrative of a worn material is unmistakable and the patterns of wear are so intricate and varying. This lends to its authentic appearance,' says Ting.

Finding reliable sources to get hold of materials, however, can be difficult, so Ting creates seasonal collections that utilize a batch of materials that they are unlikely to come across again for a limited run. Pieces such as the vintage leather belt tiles require a constant flow of used leather belts, which are hard to come by

in the hundreds. In this case the team know exactly what they are looking for in terms of quality and quantity. 'Los Angeles is a port city and a great number of discarded materials are funnelled through here before they are shipped out of the country to be reused elsewhere,' explains Ting. 'We just try to intercept them before they go. Finding a batch of materials that don't have a home is an inspiring starting point. It allows us to create a small quantity of special products that cannot be repeated.'

She adds, 'There is a certain sense of satisfaction not just in saving something from landfill, but in doing so to create something desirable and of a greater value. This is where the harsh realities of such a labour-intensive endeavour hit home. In order to stay in business you need to see a return on your investment. Some products are inherently more costly to source and process than others, but this is reflected in the quality of their appearance, which makes it worthwhile. We use a mix of different materials so we can offset the costs of different projects. This may not make the most financial sense, but it allows us to make some really interesting pieces and demonstrates how certain sets of materials can be reused in a striking and beautiful way.'

OPPOSITE:

Vintage belt rug pictured in luxury apartments at Solair Wilshire, Los Angeles. The composition for each tile or panel is carefully created in-house to ensure the correct pattern and colour balance.

Vintage belt rug detail. Ting's luxury leather flooring is made from hand-selected belts with a high grade of leather and durability.

Vintage leather belt walls made for a restaurant in
Orange County, California. The flooring and wall
panelling are a bespoke product designed for use in
private and commercial spaces.

Ting's studios source most of their vintage belts
from London, Paris and Los Angeles.

CAROLA VAN DYKE

East Sussex, United Kingdom

VINTAGE TEXTILE SCRAPS > CUSHIONS AND ANIMAL HEADS

Carola Van Dyke studied fine arts in the Netherlands and graduated with a BA in fashion illustration and textiles. After moving to England to work as a fashion illustrator and scenic artist, she set up her own line of childrenswear before launching a collection of soft furnishings. Her cushions and textile taxidermy heads are comprised of a signature patchwork style that she creates using new and old fabrics.

'I see my work as textile collage,' says Van Dyke. 'Although I have always admired traditional patchwork, my aim has always been to take it out of its predictable confines and put it into a new setting. I wanted to somehow combine my paintings and textiles, but painting directly onto textiles couldn't satisfy my need for contrasts in colours, textures and layers. It needed to be quirky, intricate and have a sense of humour, so I began to draw with scissors.'

Van Dyke picks up textile pieces wherever she goes. Vintage curtains, blankets and buttons are bought at flea markets, car boot sales, second-hand shops and antique stalls as well as online. She also sources end-of-line rolls that would otherwise be destroyed from British factories. 'I will literally buy anything I feel I can use at some point, without any particular idea in mind. Sometimes they stay unused for a few months until the right design comes up,' she says. Based in Firle, a village at the foot of the South Downs, she is also given hand-me-downs from neighbours who leave bags of unwanted material at her back door.

For her textile taxidermy heads, Van Dyke uses kilim rugs that she sources from auctions and house clearances. Everything is rigorously washed and steamed before being sorted by colour and placed in a huge cabinet. She says, 'The worn kilim rugs have had the colour walked out of them, which creates holes and fraying edges. You can see the weave underneath in a different colour, which is ideal for my big taxidermy heads. New rugs would be far too thick to manipulate around the shapes, and characterless too.'

Inspirations for Van Dyke's designs range from Turkish rug patterns to Japanese kimonos and folk art. She is also influenced by the colours used in paintings by Johannes Vermeer. She says, 'I love using fabrics that contrast with each other. The warm tweeds together with colder silks, the soft velvet with the harsh linen, fragile fabrics with pitted rough ones. You can put a whole world of colours and textures together.'

Fabrics with limited availability are not used for cushions, as the design needs to be repeatable. Instead they are saved for one-off artworks. She says, 'I need some continuity for the cushions and the taxidermy heads as people often want exactly what they have seen in a magazine or at a show.' Whenever she runs out of vintage fabrics, she is usually able to replace them with a similar material. 'It keeps the cushions exciting, fresh and limited-edition.'

She adds, 'I like seeing something that others don't see. I look at an old curtain and see a perfect texture and colour for an ear on one of my dog cushions. A new fabric wouldn't be able to give me that. I see these bits as treasure and I can't believe my luck that someone else doesn't want them. Where upcycling can go wrong is when the finished product looks dated and something from a bygone time. You have to reinvent the pieces with a fresh and imaginative approach to make them relevant.'

OPPOSITE:
Carola Van Dyke in her studio, where she
keeps all her textile scraps.

ABOVE:

Country Collection cushions. The top stitching is done on very old industrial machines dating back to the 1940s. This means some lines have to be stitched a few times, resulting in a rough-looking sketch rather than perfect embroidery.

OPPOSITE:

Textile taxidermy deer head with sika antlers, made from old tweeds and vintage fabrics. The antlers for the taxidermy heads are bought from a deer park. They are removed from the deer when they become too big, to prevent the animals from causing serious injury to each other when fighting.

OVERLEAF:

Liberty roe. Van Dyke made a series of taxidermy animals from silk scarves, commissioned by Liberty, London.

Dog cushions and textile taxidermy heads. Van Dyke mixes together hand-cut textile pieces in the same way a painter uses a palette.

FUN MAKES GOOD

Eleanor Young | Glasgow, Scotland

FOUND FURNITURE AND TEXTILE OFFCUTS > BESPOKE UPHOLSTERY

Scottish textile designer Eleanor Young graduated in embroidered textiles from the Glasgow School of Art in 2007. After completing her degree, she took up evening classes in upholstery and in 2009 set up Fun Makes Good. Young started out by developing a portfolio from a collection of found chairs that she rescued from the dump and re-covered in her signature geometric designs. As word of mouth spread, she started to revamp junk-shop finds and family heirlooms for clients and now also creates textile pieces for retail. Specializing in reworking previously unloved items of furniture with bespoke upholstery, she blends traditional techniques with a distinctive graphic aesthetic.

Frequently scouring skips, junk shops and side streets for materials, Young will often get tip-offs from friends if they see something she might be able to reuse. 'Having always enjoyed collecting things, I got into the habit of hunting for unusual materials whilst studying at art school. In the densely populated city of Glasgow, flat tenants were forever changing, which meant lots of old and tired-looking furniture would end up out on the street for people to take. I'd regularly find myself hunting around the back lanes looking in skips in the hope of finding something which could be used later,' she explains.

She adds, 'Most of the time it's just the fabric which is outdated, ripped or worn and the actual frame is in good condition. I like how you can completely transform something deemed to be rubbish with a bit of imagination. These chairs aren't designed to be chosen from a catalogue, they are items with a history and a story that will keep going.'

All of the projects Young embarks on try to employ a policy of zero waste. Scraps from previous work are used in new products and upholstery. This means oddly shaped pieces of fabric will often help to inform new designs. Keeping boxes of colour-coded leftover scraps, no piece of fabric is too small, 'I can create whole sections of fabric from almost nothing,' she says. This is the technique she uses to make her After Upholstery (AU) cushions, which means that no two are ever the same.

She says, 'Years ago, people had a greater understanding of using everything until it fell apart as there was no other option. The creation of patchwork quilts goes back centuries. I like the way these items were treated as heirlooms, created by family members, filled with stories and handed on down through the generations. I hope some of my pieces will be treated in the same way and loved for many years. It is important to show consumers that they can still buy new things, but new things that have been made in a mindful way. I think people are starting to see that upcycling is not just for hobbyists. Those with design knowledge are now creating desirable objects from waste.'

OPPOSITE:

Slagelse Møbelvaerk Boomerang Chairs set of 6 dining chairs, each with an individual design. The brief was to keep parts of the existing vinyl and replace damaged parts with new vinyl pieces. The design of the upholstery was informed by the shape of the furniture, complementing the boomerang curves of the existing chairs.

ABOVE:
Eleanor Young in her studio with Boomerang chair.

BELOW:
G-Plan Alfresco chair re-upholstered in a flecked tweed fabric made locally on the Isle of Bute.

OPPOSITE:
After Upholstery limited-edition cushions are made from hand-dyed cotton satin, bute wool, tweed, wool, felt and corduroy offcuts from previous upholstery commissions. The reclaimed armchair was restored in 100% wool tweed with purple suede and leather-covered buttons. The woodwork was also stripped back and varnished with a dark oak finish.

METAL

+BRAUER

Bruno Lefèvre-Brauer | Paris, France

Bruno Lefèvre-Brauer, also known as +Brauer, has worked as a graphic designer, sculptor and painter for over 20 years. *Viva la roboluciòn!* is a collection of robot sculptures made from vintage mechanical parts found abandoned in workshops and garages. The robots are showcased at +Brauer Gallery, located in the Marais area of Paris, a neighbourhood renowned for its industrial and artisanal past.

'Since childhood I've been influenced by novels, comics and American sci-fi series. I admire the magical world of *Metropolis* by Fritz Lang and the vastness of *2001: A Space Odyssey* by Stanley Kubrick,' says Lefèvre-Brauer. 'I have also always loved outsider art and the instinctive energy that emerges from it. Artists have always appropriated objects in their work, without necessarily considering the environment whilst doing so.'

Having collected Japanese robots for 20 years, Lefèvre-Brauer created his first robot sculpture around 10 years ago, a simple metal case topped by an insulator with keys for arms. With the complexity involved in assembling lights from recycled materials, each robot presents a new challenge and Lefèvre-Brauer has developed new methods to obtain the results he is looking for. In addition to using techniques such as sawing, cutting, welding, screwing and burnishing, the most complex part is the electrical process that brings each robot to life. 'With each sculpture, I sharpen my electrical skills,' he says.

Lefèvre-Brauer has been gathering materials to make robots for several years. The collection is comprised of objects bought second-hand or from scrap merchants as well as items found abandoned on the streets. He also has a network of artisans who bring him objects they have picked up. He says, 'With such a large stock of material, there are no limits on my imagination. At times an idea for a new sculpture pops into my head at the sight of a single object.'

The robots begin as sketches on paper, after which different objects are assembled on the floor to create the desired shape. 'This allows me to refine the sculpture, adapt it to the parts I have at my disposal and find out what new parts I need to complete it,' says Lefèvre-Brauer. 'Some sculptures remain in progress in my workshop for months until I finally find the missing parts.' After working out how to set up the lighting, which is specifically tailored to each robot, he cuts openings that form windows in the metal. Once the electrical network is set up, he can begin assembling and welding. 'The main challenge is to assemble materials that are not meant to be put together. Each part reveals its own constraints and adding light to it makes the task even more complicated. I go through many tests before implementing the electrical element,' he explains.

Lefèvre-Brauer's robots are in part born out of a poetic resistance to consumption. He says, 'I choose vintage objects that have an industrial past, that have been marked by time and whose patina has been moulded by years of manual use. I'm so keen on old industrial objects that I don't think I would be able to create things out of recent or modern materials. It's always interesting to talk to children about upcycling. They show a great interest in art made out of recycled objects and I think upcycling in art conveys a positive image for recycling in general.'

OPPOSITE:
Viva la roboluciòn! Phil, 2010. Various mechanical parts with the body made from a truck battery charger.

Viva la roboluciòn! Commodor, 2013. Named after the Commodor electrical box brand, the legs are made from the stand of a darkroom photo enlarger. Fuel tank caps from vintage cars and motorcycles let the rays of light through.

Viva la roboluciòn! Horton, 2009. The mechanical parts include a cinema's condensing unit and a winding car-window handle for the nose.

Foreground: *Alfred*, 2010. Background: *Youri* light, 2012, and *Taxi* light, 2008, also by Lefèvre-Brauer. *Taxi* is made from a taxi sign sourced from Rome.

YESTERDAY RECLAIMED

Roque Castro | Virginia, United States

SALVAGED TAILGATES, FARMING IMPLEMENTS AND BARN WOOD > FURNITURE

Following in the footsteps of a family accomplished in the arts, Roque Castro, founder of Yesterday Reclaimed, started his design education at Virginia Tech. He then embarked on a 10-year corporate career in investment banking until 2010, when he and his wife decided to relocate their family from the outskirts of Manhattan to the horse and cattle country of central Virginia. During normal business hours Castro works as head of sales for a software firm. Now, with plenty of work space, fresh country air and years of pent-up design ideas, he spends his free time picking through farm scrapyards, peeling boards off old barns and designing a product line that has become Yesterday Reclaimed.

'Most people call it a labour of love, but we like to call it therapy,' says Castro. What started as a hobby to escape a high-pressure career in financial services has expanded into a design and fabrication business with a growing product line, located in Culpeper, Virginia. Castro's design inspiration comes from the industrial and agrarian lifestyle of the region. His love of farming stems from his childhood on a Black Angus beef farm, where he spent time helping his grandfather and uncle on their Ayrshire dairy operation.

Pieces by Yesterday Reclaimed are created from salvaged materials such as hardwoods from old barns and steel from farming implements. Materials range from mechanical parts from an old forage wagon to the metal support membrane of a concrete silo. 'Each piece carries a history backed by blood, sweat and tears,' says Castro. 'We tend to draw inspiration from the gnarliest, most dramatic parts of the machinery – large sprockets, gears, cogs and internal parts with an edge. From there we like to soften the hard steel with reclaimed wood, often sourced from dilapidated barns or from lumberyards that specialize in antique hard woods.'

He continues, 'There is truth to the old adage "they don't make them like they used to." Many of the industrial components we repurpose into furniture are from an era where equipment and machinery were bulkier and heavier than they are today. Many of the steel parts we find have been replaced with composite, lighter materials that just wouldn't make for as interesting a product.'

In addition to the rust, termites and trials of Mother Nature, Castro has also come up against the issue of storing the salvaged materials. He says, 'Experience has taught me to be more cautious when acquiring materials in bulk unless I truly feel that there is a commercial market for the end result. I once purchased hundreds of vintage Tonka Trucks to be repurposed into bookends, only to find the idea didn't have a mass-market appeal. It has taken me years to get rid of those damn toy trucks!'

He adds, 'The nostalgic aspect of upcycling found objects into furniture initially attracted me to the craft. I am a history buff at heart. I love researching the background and prior life of the more interesting materials that we get our hands on. Many people assume that it was the earth-friendly aspect of upcycling that motivated us to launch the business, but that wasn't the case in the beginning. Now it's an equal balance of nostalgia and eco-friendly motivations.'

OPPOSITE:

Blue Collar bench, made from the tailgate of a vintage 1970s red Ford pickup truck, framed in square tubing steel and skinned with antique red oak barn wood.

Castro's team reclaim parts from abandoned farming implements that have been left to rot in back acres of old farmland, also known as boneyards. Castro works with a network of salvage yards and a team of 'pickers' that travel up and down the eastern seaboard of the United States.

Sid Vicious side table made from the upper roller of a 1970s John Deere model 3800 Forage Harvester. The steel-toothed roller has been left intact and is welded to a plough disc for support. The table top is formed from a vintage wooden spool end sourced from an industrial warehouse clearout.

The Man Beater end table, made from the gnarly moving parts of a forage wagon, the unloading beater. The steel was salvaged from a 1970s Coby chuck wagon used on a farm in central Virginia. The reclaimed wood for the shelves came from a 120-year-old corn crib.

Chevy Blue Collar Bench made from a 1960s baby-blue pickup tailgate sourced from a vintage auto scrapyard in North Carolina. The pine tongue-and-groove wood was reclaimed from the flooring of a turn-of-the-century house in central Virginia.

THE RAG AND BONE MAN

Paul Firbank | London, United Kingdom

Contemporary craftsman Paul Firbank established The Rag and Bone Man in his native borough of Hackney, East London, in 2011. With a lifelong respect for the innate beauty of quality engineering, he fills his workshop with time-honoured machinery including a 1920s jennying machine made on London's Euston Road, a 1950s Myford lathe and a British 1940s New Progress pillar drill. Firbank originally studied metalwork with the aim of customizing push bikes and motorcycles. With his strong perfectionist streak, experience in altering his own machines gave him new skills and techniques. Working from his studio, he now re-crafts aged engine parts, machinery and modern scrap into bespoke furniture, lighting and accessories.

Aged machinery, vehicle parts and modern scrap otherwise destined for the melting pot are collected from Firbank's favourite London scrapyards and grease shops. He often comes across new places to get hold of scrap while exploring on his bike. Back in the studio, much of his work is a process of restoration using traditional metalwork techniques. Hours are spent cutting, stripping, cleaning, turning, welding and polishing.

Scraps of history, each component has its own story. Firbank says, 'The scraps often come from a period of manufacture and engineering where things were built to last but were also beautifully designed. I initially used scrap out of necessity in order to find affordable materials but when I started researching the components, I was so inspired by their industrial history that I chose to make them the focus of my work.'

Firbank channels the character and quirks of every piece of scrap he finds into new, functional forms. The shapes and mechanisms of each part suggest a potential adaptation, so he responds to the qualities of the materials, rather than working against their parameters. Because the components are so diverse, each can lend something different to a potential new design. The combinations of these components also make each piece original and often unrepeatable. 'Casting is a costly process, so finding pre-existing metal materials offers an opportunity that might otherwise be unaffordable,' he explains. He adds, 'The current reputation of upcycling is dominated by DIY activity. As a result you tend to see a lot of quick-fix "side-cycling", products being repurposed with the intention of being resourceful but to a standard that may not stand the test of time.' In contrast Firbank shows a commitment to building high-quality pieces and enforces a careful process of documenting their provenance by giving each work its own unique number. His bespoke creations bring the traditions of the 19th-century rag-and-bone man into a contemporary context with a unique style of craftsmanship that fuses the past with the present.

OPPOSITE:
DL0010, a desk lamp made using various connecting rods usually used in automotive piston engines, including one by the British sports car manufacturer TVR. The piece also incorporates a cutter holder from a moulding machine, tap handles and an engine cover for the shade.

OVERLEAF:
WL0009-13, from a series of five wall lamps made from vintage plumbing parts and Firbank's signature cut fire extinguisher shades.

PREVIOUS PAGE CLOCKWISE:

WL0009-13, from a series of five wall lamps made from vintage plumbing parts and Firbank's signature cut fire extinguisher shades.

Firbank at work in the studio. Once complete, each product is meticulously archived and bears its own hand-stamped tag with a unique serial number and completion date.

CL0001. The central body of this chandelier is the crank case front cover of a Lycoming R680 radial engine. Eighteen copper arms extend from where the push rods used to be. Light bowls at the end of each arm have been made from fire extinguishers that have been cut, stripped and polished into two different shapes. There is also a downlight running through where the propeller shaft would have been (see also pages 108–09).

ABOVE:

FU0007, a bar stool created from a vintage gearbox, engine pulley and a rare tractor seat.

TL0009, a table lamp featuring a polished engine cover and the negative metal waste from a wire-eroding machine.

OPPOSITE CLOCKWISE:

Firbank in his East London workshop. The mechanical parts and scrap metal utilized in his work would otherwise be destined for the furnace.

CH0001–8 golf club clothes hangers. A series of clothes hangers handmade from unwanted golf clubs, a vast number of which get thrown away every year. Each hanger is unique in its combination of clubs, serial number and production date, which is hand-stamped onto each frame.

Firbank uses a die grinder to hone and polish the scrap metal.

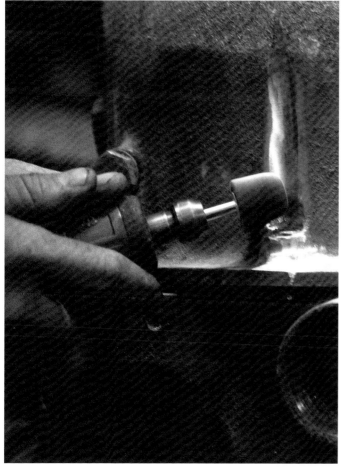

FACARO

Carolina Fontoura Alzaga | California, United States

USED BICYCLE CHAINS, RIMS AND COGS > CHANDELIERS

After initially studying painting and digital art in Denver, Colorado, since 2008 multidisciplinary artist Carolina Fontoura Alzaga has been developing *The CONNECT Series*: functional sculptures made from bike chains, rims and cogs that resemble elegant and meticulously handcrafted chandeliers. With materials sourced from abandoned bikes in junk yards and bike shop dumpsters in downtown LA, Alzaga transforms the discarded and industrial into something surprisingly delicate and luxurious.

The first chandelier was made at a time when Alzaga was heavily influenced by trash art and bike punk culture but was in fact the result of a semantic mistake. After seeing some kitchenware hanging from a makeshift pot rack made from an old bicycle rim, she was initially inspired to make a mobile from bicycle parts. Through trial and error, however, she mastered a technique that enabled her to create a cascading effect with all the elegance of a traditional Victorian chandelier, and so *The CONNECT Series* was born.

With all her chandeliers, Alzaga's biggest challenge lies in trying to approximate perfection with an imperfect material. The bike chains may appear as though they are naturally meant to be put together, but achieving their effortless quality requires dexterity. Alzaga has had to learn various techniques to find her way around the complex system of chains within each piece. 'To maintain the integrity of the concept, *The CONNECT Series* must solely be comprised of used bike parts. It is the rigidity and flexibility of the bike chains that determine how each piece is composed. In order to work in small spaces behind layers and layers of chains I've had to develop the ability to see with my fingertips,' she says.

Inspiration for Alzaga's work ranges from the wire sculptures of Japanese-American artist Ruth Asawa to the catenaries found in bridges, arches and architecture. Her work is also influenced by geometry, the mandalas of Hindu and Buddhist symbolism and the patterning and sequencing informed by rhythm in music. She says, 'Even when I was 16, whilst listening to 'Phoenix' by Daft Punk, I felt the urge to draw a musical notation of the song in my own symbols and patterns.'

She adds, 'Since childhood I've been struck by weathered textures that enable you to see the materialization of time. I'm attracted to the notion of making the invisible visible by imbuing it with value. I think utilizing reclaimed materials highlights the importance of ingenuity, reinvention, resourcefulness and the beauty of nuanced imperfection in a world that imposes standards of perfection and propagates disposability.'

Dedicated to finding creative solutions to excessive waste, *The CONNECT Series* is informed by principles of social and environmental sustainability. Alzaga says, 'A society that propagates planned obsolescence is doomed: it's short-sighted and ultimately suicidal. I hope that more people realize this and consider how they are contributing to either the solution or the problem, because you cannot be neutral. Movements are cyclical by nature and it may be that upcycling is one of many trends that come and go, but I expect the future will see more and more sophisticated upcycling propositions.'

OPPOSITE:
Caroline Fontoura Alzaga with *CONNECT 13*, 2012, for Eastside Genéve store, Geneva, Switzerland.

OPPOSITE:
Alzaga's materials are sourced from around 150 bike
shop dumpsters around the greater Los Angeles area
as well as junk- and scrapyards in downtown LA.

ABOVE:
CONNECT 18, 2012.
Imperial Restaurant, Portland, Oregon.

CONNECT 21c, 2014.
Private client, Amsterdam, The Netherlands.

ABOVE:

Painting bike rims in a ventilated spray booth. Aside from welding, the making process is moderately low-tech as the sourcing, sketching and production is all done by hand. When working on large-scale pieces Alzaga works with a structural engineer and structural welder.

OPPOSITE:

Detail of *CONNECT 18*.

WILLEM HEEFFER

Helsinki, Finland

USED WASHING-MACHINE DRUMS AND TIN CANS > LIGHTING

Willem Heeffer studied product design at Design Academy Eindhoven in The Netherlands. After working in Dublin, Ireland, for seven years as a product and interior designer, he opened up his own workshop in Helsinki. Taking old materials out of context and reusing them in unexpected ways, Heeffer wants his viewers to see his pieces as beautiful products before they discover the history behind them. 'Only then can they be viewed as design pieces rather than trash,' he says.

'In a time of mass consumption where products have a short lifespan, we are looking for pieces with a meaning, a story or a history. I like to show the reasons and the processes behind how an object is made. This gives the owner a better understanding of the product and allows them to form a much stronger connection with it. In turn, the products will be loved and looked after and will stay with their owners for longer. Recycled materials show the scars of life and have stories to tell. This I cannot recreate from scratch.'

From Marcel Duchamp's famous upturned urinal *Fountain* (1917) to the concrete drainpipe hotel rooms at Das Park Hotel in Bottrop, Germany, Heeffer has always been interested in the readymade. He believes, however, that there is often confusion between readymade and upcycled products. 'I think an important overlooked criterion for upcycling is that the object you use must have served its purpose before you upcycle it,' he says, adding, 'I believe good design is mindful design. Ecology and ethics should form an integral part of this. So I always try to limit waste, recycle wherever possible and bring new life to discarded materials. We should however be careful about thinking that sustainability is the only solution. As futurist Christopher Barnatt pointed out in an article in *The Guardian* (October 2013), "we should start focusing on how we can least painfully deconstruct our consumer society and transition to a world in which we consume things less and value things more."'

Heeffer will often salvage objects and instantly know what to do with them, but he also collects pieces without knowing their future purpose. In addition to his lights made from powder-coated washing machine drums, he has furnished several Helsinki diners and restaurants with his lamps made from Heinz baked beans cans and cooking oil tins. He says, 'Upcycled products are often more expensive than mass-produced items as there is a lot of labour involved and they are usually one-off limited editions. I do however think it is a very clever move for agencies, restaurants, hotels and stores to integrate upcycled design into their interiors. It communicates uniqueness, authenticity and mindfulness, all the values a company should want to be associated with.'

OPPOSITE:

Heinz beans can lights and KTC oil drum lights at Midhill Restaurant in Linnanmäki, Helsinki. This was Heeffer's first big upcycling project for top chef Hans Välimäki's American diner. The designers Martina Rosenqvist and Vera Öller colour-matched the interior to the lamps, made from locally sourced Heinz baked beans cans and cooking oil drums.

Heinz beans can lights. The tins are everyday waste collected from local cafés and restaurants.

ABOVE:

Drum lights made from powder-coated washing-
machine drums are produced in a range of colours.
The lamps are handmade with locally sourced
recycled materials.

OPPOSITE:

Heeffer designed the interior for the Mandala travel
agency and tour operator in Helsinki. Drum lights
have been powder-coated in the agency's signature
colours. Window seating, wall cladding and stools
have been made from reclaimed wood. The wood
was supplied by waste solution company SITA.

ALEX RANDALL DESIGN

London, United Kingdom

Alex Randall is an award-winning British artist and designer renowned for her use of unconventional materials to create remarkable lighting. In addition to using salvaged and antique objects, she is famed for the use of taxidermy in her work, in particular the Rat Swarm lamp, a nightmarish piece made from dead vermin. After studying sculpture at Chelsea School of Art, Alex launched her career as a lighting artist in 2006 with her Bakelite telephone lamp. The following year her pieces made their way into prestigious London stores including Liberty and Harvey Nichols. Her work has been installed in hotels, boutiques and private residences internationally, ranging from Lane Crawford in Hong Kong to Ken Fulk in San Francisco.

The desired aesthetic for The Blues Kitchen in Shoreditch was that of a fashionable lived-in bar with an industrial edge. Inspired by steampunk, the interior nods to the deep southern states of the USA. 'Shoreditch hums with moustachioed trendsetters, so achieving the right look was very important. It's the biggest bar in the area, so the lighting had to create intimate pockets to break up the space,' says Randall. In a project such as this, the first job is a scouting mission which must be carried out before any design processes or meetings with the client have taken place. Having worked closely with various antique dealers and reclamation yards around the UK for many years, Randall knows who to call to find an extra-special item. With the knowledge of what she can get hold of, she creates a fast mock-up of all the available options for the client; this has to happen quickly, as items can often go before the client has approved them. The next stage is to purchase the items before creating more detailed designs.

Randall relishes the opportunity to reuse something with a personal history that would otherwise be seen as waste. She says, 'I believe good design has to go beyond the physical. Using found and reclaimed materials gives me a starting point for a really great story. The way I begin designing is to look at the history of the piece and the emotive response that it creates. It would be virtually impossible to design something before you have the items to hand as there is no guarantee you will be able to find them. This is one of the things that appeals to me and makes the item all the more special and unique.'

She adds, 'New design can be an extremely wasteful process and it is this notion of waste that has led me to use all sorts of different materials in my designs. From culled animals to discarded barrels, waste in the UK is a fascinating resource and one that has inspired all sorts of different movements. Across the globe we are producing waste at an unacceptable level and we need to rethink the way we create and discard items. I don't believe that even recycling as we currently know it is the most efficient way to reuse waste. Upcycling is an ancient practice which is becoming increasingly relevant to the contemporary world. Long before IKEA, we made all our essential items, fixed them, changed them and brought them back into use. It is only the modern throwaway generation that has broken this cycle. Now that we are looking more carefully at how a desire for new things is impacting on the environment, upcycling seems more essential than ever.'

OPPOSITE:
Lights made from burnished gas tubes create an industrial aesthetic.

Pendants made from antique wash coppers
lined with copper leaf. Coppers were originally
used as washing tubs in outhouses during the
Victorian and Edwardian eras.

Lamps made from salvaged plumb fittings
burnished with copper leaf highlight the rough
texture of the walls behind.

ABOVE:

Pendants made from antique fire hydrants.
Lighting was used to create cosy pockets of
space and to demarcate the different areas of
the bar.

Twisted block lamps made from twisted steel
with an oak base.

OPPOSITE:

Chandeliers made from gramophone horns and
a steel frame.

RAFINESSE & TRISTESSE

Karin Yilmaz-Egger and Petra Schultz | Berlin, Germany, and Bern, Switzerland

OLIVE-OIL TINS > FURNITURE AND ACCESSORIES

After Karin Yilmaz-Egger and Petra Schultz successfully crafted a toy miniature kitchen from an old olive-oil tin for one of their own children, their friends urged them to develop more products. In 2006 they founded Rafinesse & Tristesse and have been creating products for children and the home ever since. Their breakthrough came in 2008 when they won an award at the Ambiente design fair in Frankfurt, after which they could no longer keep up with the demand for their stools made from olive-oil tins. With the team still growing, all their products are handmade in Berlin and also Bern, Switzerland, where they collaborate closely with several social service programmes. These include Triva, a work programme for drug addicts in Bern, and USE, a work programme for people with special needs in Berlin.

All Rafinesse & Tristesse products revolve around the concept of using as many recycled items as possible. Olive-oil tins from wholesale traders in Bern and Berlin and vintage tins from flea markets are washed and reworked into artistic, playful and high-quality pieces. 'I first fell in love with these tins when I was working in restaurants as a student,' says Schultz. 'They have nice nostalgic design and it's a strong material. I have a big affinity with reusing

old things and have always reworked furniture to give it a second life. It's incredible how much we throw away in order to buy something new.'

In addition to the popular Tin Tuffet stools made from upholstered olive-oil tins, Rafinesse & Tristesse have a colourful portfolio of products that includes bar stools made from two tins stacked on top of each other. The stools are strengthened from the inside with wood to make them stable. Seat benches made from maple or plywood with tins forming built-in storage also form part of the collection, as do steam-rolled tins that are turned into magnetic key hangers, paper roll holders, coat racks and notice boards with recycled Höfbrau 'crown cap' magnets.

'Although the prices of handmade upcycled products struggle to keep up with the market prices of mass-produced items, we believe an appreciation for this philosophy and type of production is already here,' says Yilmaz-Egger. 'The temptation to buy plenty and cheap is still big,' she adds. 'Our aim is to strengthen consciousness so that people think before throwing something away. Abundance and avarice poison our nature. We are always looking for alternative solutions.'

OPPOSITE:
Rafinesse & Tristesse products on display at their store in Bern, Switzerland. Tin Tuffet stools are made from upholstered used olive-oil tins. Their first ever products, Frizzle Sizzle and Splish Splash, are miniature kitchens and kitchen sinks for children, all made from recycled tins and jar lids.

CLOCKWISE:

Seat bench. Each one is unique, as all the tins are matched with different fabrics. All the tins have handles for easy removal and felt pads to protect them from slipping and scratching floors.

A corner of the studio in Berlin. Rafinesse & Tristesse steam-roll used olive-oil tins to create products such as magnetic notice boards, coat hangers and key hangers.

Rafinesse & Tristesse flowerpots on the terrace at Kater Holzig restaurant, Berlin.

Yilmaz-Egger's daughters Elif and Finja sitting on the Tin Tuffet stools at the beach.

OPPOSITE:

Rafinesse & Tristesse produce made-to-order freestanding sideboards, shelving and storage units, all made from used olive-oil tins.

GLASS AND CERAMICS

ATTENDANT CAFÉ

Peter Tomlinson and Ben Russell | London, United Kingdom

VICTORIAN PORCELAIN URINALS AND TILES > CAFÉ INTERIOR

Located on Foley Street in the heart of media and advertising hub Fitzrovia is a former Victorian public toilet that ceased operations in the 1970s. A private landlord bought the abandoned gentlemen's convenience from Westminster Council in 1986 with the intention of turning it into a printing works, but it lay dormant for another 15 years. Peter Tomlinson and Ben Russell first spotted the 'To Let' sign outside the disused lavatory when they were drinking outside the nearby Crown and Sceptre pub. At the time, the gloomy stairs leading underground were filled with rubbish. Undeterred, it wasn't long before Tomlinson took redundancy from his marketing job and invested £100,000 in transforming it into Attendant, a 390m² subterranean café. After two years of planning and restoration, a thorough deep clean and a complete makeover, the café opened in February 2013. A year later, it was bought by its current owners, Bosh McKeown and Ryan De Oliveira.

Although some might have considered gutting the place to be the most practical approach, and one that certainly would have allowed for more seating, the vision was to keep as many original features as possible. Using an architect to help design the layout, Tomlinson and Russell did all the interior design themselves and came up with the innovative idea to upcycle the original Doulton & Co. urinals. Manufactured at the Lambeth factory on the Thames in the late 19th century, the urinals were transformed into a unique coffee bench with individual booths for customers to sit at.

After being sanitized with a jet wash and with the water supply reinstated from Thames Water, the former lavatory retains a couple of original cisterns and all its original wall and floor tiles, apart from those covering the bar and drains. It also still has a vintage hand dryer on the wall as well as the original teak door to the toilet attendant's office, which now provides extra seating. The service bar is located where the original cubicles once stood, now serving exotic teas, gourmet sandwiches and coffee from Caravan Roastery in King's Cross. Attractive original cast iron railings around the upper structure are owned by the council. The roof, which was added later, creates a striking feature at street level, and fold-down benches allow for an outdoor seating area. The award-winning café now has queues that wind out of the door and up the stairs every day during lunchtime.

'Upcycling is exciting and innovative,' says Tomlinson. 'Looking at something with a different perspective requires confidence in the creative process. Most people won't be able to "see" your vision until it's finished, then all of a sudden everyone can see the obvious. Creating London's first coffee shop in a toilet didn't sound good at the pitch stage, but Attendant will continue to wow people because it was a perfect concept and people love peculiar things.'

The café retains virtually all its original Victorian floor and wall tiles from the 1890s. New tiles to cover the drains were sourced from the same Spanish manufacturer that supplied the original tiles when the lavatory was first built.

ABOVE:
Located in the media hub of Goodge Street, the café is perfectly situated for workers to pick up their morning espresso.

OPPOSITE CLOCKWISE:
The original hatch where customers would pay the toilet attendant.

The original teak door to the toilet attendant's office.

Next to the imposing cast iron structure, pull-down benches offer customers outdoor seating.

OVERLEAF:
The porcelain urinal bench creates booths for customers to sit at. The Doulton & Co. porcelain urinals were transformed into a feature coffee bar. Kelly green bar stools give the space a pop of colour and were chosen to match the original green Victorian tiles. A couple of the original cisterns have also been kept as a decorative feature.

JULI BOLAÑOS-DURMAN

Edinburgh, Scotland

USED MANUFACTURED GLASS AND DISCARDED BLOWN GLASS > SCULPTURE

Juli Bolaños-Durman is an award-winning designer and maker originally from Costa Rica. With a background in graphic design, she moved to Scotland to do an MFA in glass at Edinburgh College of Art. After graduating with distinction, she went on to be artist-in-residence there. Bolaños-Durman's *Ode to Intuición* series is an exploration of preciousness and play. She says, 'Preciousness is not only to be found in the value or quality of the materials but more so in what they represent. I find myself choosing and treasuring things that tell a story and carry emotional connections. Whether they are beautiful antiques or random, ordinary pieces of glass, I see potential in what they could become.'

The *Ode to Intuición* series gives a precious appearance to found everyday manufactured glass such as jam jars, syrup bottles and liqueur bottles through a process of cold working and engraving. In some cases Bolaños-Durman also reuses blown glass from students' discarded glass piles at the art college. Cutting up the glass into components, she plays around with the construction of the new object before smoothing, engraving and polishing. The parts are then glued together to create non-functional, sculptural vessels.

Bolaños-Durman's free and intuitive process of making is inspired by Donald Schön's theory of reflective practice. She says, 'Relying on feeling, response and adjustment, I allow myself to improvise, play and interact with the components without any preconceived notions. Not trying too hard to control the creative flow results in pieces that are completely raw and unique.'

As part of her research, she invited an audience to engage with the materials in a mix-and-match workshop. With 50 glass components laid out on a grid, volunteers were given five minutes to create three non-functional vessels whilst wearing a GoPro head video camera that recorded the selection process. She says, 'I try to remind myself of childhood curiosity and how, as children, we were more connected to our intuition and were able to play freely without boundaries. When the pressure is off, play is an unlimited source of new ideas.'

She adds, 'Besides the obvious benefits, I enjoy reusing materials because it is a personal challenge. As an artist, I have a certain sensibility in being able to see the potential of ordinary objects, to give them a second chance and transform them into precious pieces. It wouldn't be possible to make my work without reclaiming materials. My collections come to life and have a personality precisely because they are a combination of carefully curated and transformed objects. If they were completely controlled they would have a different feel.'

OPPOSITE:
Ode to Intuición series, 2013, *Queen of the Night.*

OPPOSITE:
Flying Nun.

ABOVE:
Ode to Intuición series, 2013, from left: *Queen Bishop,*
Juana La Cubana, Aubergine Esmeralda, Fabergé
and *La Virgencita.*

ESTHER DERKX

Utrecht, Netherlands

After studying 3D design, Esther Derkx became inspired to learn more about traditional craft. She expanded her skills by working in both a ceramics company and a screenprinting company. In 2000 she started her career as an independent designer and artist in Utrecht and now owns a studio at Uranus Cultuurlab, a collective with 30 other creative companies, some of which she collaborates with on a regular basis.

In the same year, Derkx launched her own line of Improved! china. Vintage cups and saucers, plates, coffee pots and glassware are all screenprinted with her own decals, which are deliberately designed to complement the original print in a way that creates humour and surprise. Influenced by Dutch designers such as Tejo Remy and René Veenhuizen, she uses common techniques for new applications and has developed a range of unique products made from worthless materials, including lighting made from redundant street lamps.

Derkx has a small team of friends and family who source china from flea markets and second-hand stores. She also works with a large waste-processing company that provides her with porcelain.

'I am always looking for quality products that are incomplete or outdated and have therefore been discarded,' she says. 'The things companies and individuals see as waste surprises me all the time. I was raised to be very resourceful and economical. Being able to see the value in reclaimed materials was influenced by my travels around West Africa. I saw how every little thing can be repaired or reused in some way. I also grew up as the daughter of two environmental activists who made me aware of all the value that surrounds us in nature.'

The characters pictured on Improved! china are yogi, dancers, bodybuilders and athletes. Derkx says, 'The traditional flowers and decorative decor transform into a landscape in which the characters move around. They become a tattoo on the arm of a body builder, or decorative lines that create a sense of speed around a running athlete. Reclaimed objects have a history that can be read in the material. I like to build a new story upon the old one and give the product or material a new twist. I think what makes the Improved! china attractive is that you can recognize the era that the first version came from.'

Improved! china. Derkx transfers images of yogi, dancers, bodybuilders and athletes onto vintage china. Cups, saucers and a large round platter with elaborate gold detailing, pictured here, were made especially for an exhibition about decadence at Keramiekmuseum Princessehof in Leeuwarden, The Netherlands.

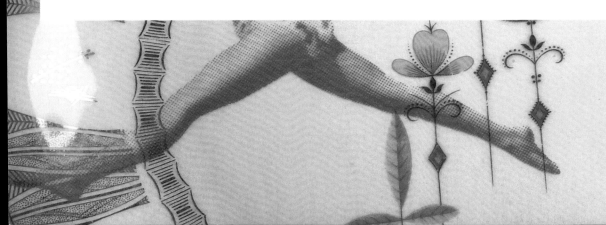

The male figure appears to be jumping off the edge
of the plate, giving velocity to the decoration.
Humour is introduced with the positioning
of the flowers: is he nude or not?

The floral decoration was originally designed to be at the bottom of the plate. Now, the scene is transformed and the figure appears to be escaping from a magical wonderland.

BEAT UP CREATIONS

Angela Rossi | California, United States

VINTAGE CHINA > REWORKED

Angela Rossi was born in Hollywood and raised in Los Angeles, California. She is a self-taught outsider artist who works with recycled, abused, broken and forgotten items. In addition to making raw assemblage sculptures and mixed media portraits, Rossi creates Altered Antique Plates, second-hand vintage china reworked with contemporary designs. Highly influenced by pop culture, anthropomorphism and the urban style of Los Angeles, her playful approach comes from the juxtaposition of highbrow classicism with an injection of the surreal. She describes her taste as 'a mix of the traditional with the unconventional'.

Rossi's mother was an avid antique collector and dealer. When she retired, she began to get rid of various bits and pieces, many of which were old plates. Rossi says, 'Made from delicate porcelain, with their hand-painted details and gold accents, I thought the plates were beautiful, but they didn't match my modern, urban style. Instead of rendering them useless, I decided to transform something traditionally formal into something fun and contemporary with a humorous edge.'

Rossi sources her plates from antique shops, thrift stores and house clearances. She says, 'There is an unnecessary overproduction and excess of discarded and unwanted plates. Thrift stores are piled high with them.' Depending on each plate's original design, Rossi matches it to one of her mixed media portraits. These are made using a combination of hand collage and digital rendering. Her portfolio of characters began with the Picture Day collection, a series of dogs and cats in 1960s clothing and geeky glasses having their school photo taken. These were initially made as gifts for friends and family and were never originally intended for resale, but she continued to find more and more retro plates with atomic motifs that seemed to perfectly complement her '60s-style portraits.

The Renaissance series continues the anthropomorphic theme that Rossi describes as 'both a tribute to and a rebellion against classical portraiture'. The designs are reworked from forgotten and obscure 16th-, 17th-, 18th- and 19th-century portraits and are given appropriately high-status names, such as Sir Ovis Aries, Brutus the Boxer and Queen Nadira of Persia. The character Marquise de Struthio, for example, is an interpretation of *Portrait of a Woman, possibly Sara Wolphaerts van Diemen* by 17th-century Dutch painter Frans Hals.

Rossi also incorporates macabre characters into her work, such as zombies and circus freaks. She says, 'I love the contrast between the old and new, soft and hard, pretty and ugly. Working with offbeat characters, punks, freaks, monsters, rebels and sci-fi somehow just seems to work with dainty and delicate hand-painted florals.'

OPPOSITE:
Timeless Tiger Portrait plate, made from a
vintage Noritake porcelain plate.

LEFT TO RIGHT:

The Snake Lady Portrait plate from the Circus Freak series, made from a vintage English Crown Ducal Ware plate with a scalloped edge.

Yoda and the Nymphs plate, made from an antique French Jean Pouyat-Limoges porcelain plate, *c.* 1906–22. It features a poppy motif in soft pastel pink and mint green.

Marquise de Struthio Portrait plate, made from a vintage Black Knight porcelain plate featuring a heavy gold gilt double crest and floral motif.

Katie, Kindergarten Portrait plate, made from a vintage Homer Laughlin 'Eggshell Georgian' plate.

Portrait of Brutus plate, made from a vintage Furstenberg porcelain charger plate with a burnt sienna crest.

PAPER AND PLASTIC

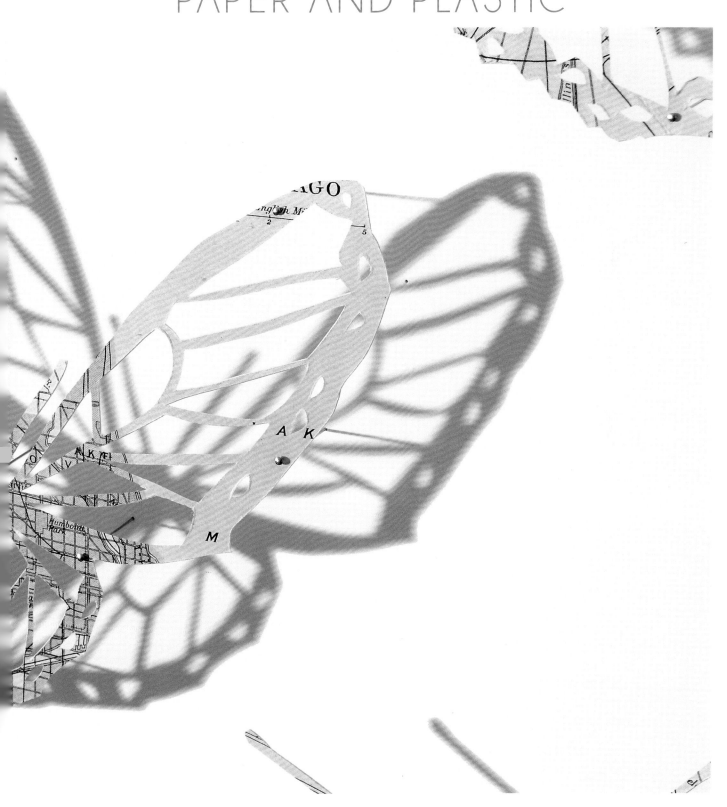

ATELIER BOMDESIGN

Michael Bom | Rotterdam, The Netherlands

Michael Bom grew up in Cape Town, South Africa, and has lived in Holland for 25 years. After studying at the Willem de Kooning Academie in Rotterdam, Bom started his own graphic design studio, Atelier Bomdesign, with his partner Antoinet Deurloo in 1993. After some years his creative course steered towards developing handmade products from used materials, including a series of lamps produced from used books, maps and paper.

'I am particularly inspired by furniture designers from the first half of the previous century century such as Bruno Munari, Gerrit Rietveld, Ilmari Tapiovaara and Cees Braakman. They were very creative with minimal means and materials,' says Bom. Often choosing pieces that have typographic elements in them, the first object Bom designed was Billbirdhouse, a bird box made from wooden sign boards and a cupboard handle to perch on. 'I always try to keep my designs pure with simple forms. I also make the construction visible so that it informs the aesthetic of the design,' he adds. Reclaiming materials has always played a big role in Bom's

life. As a student all his furniture was made from found materials salvaged from the street, including a bathroom shelving unit made from a fridge door. 'My father was a great teacher who re-used simple materials to create beautiful objects. In the '60s he made his own furniture from shipping crate wood and, when he was older, he made beautiful candle holders from used tin cans,' he says.

The materials Bom uses for his lamps are found in his direct surroundings, and are chosen because he sees a quality in them that can be used again. He says, 'Materials such as books, Venetian blinds or vinyl records are easy to find on the street or in thrift stores. I take the materials from their familiar context, study their qualities and apply them in an unusual manner. I am always searching for new possibilities to transform a book, a piece which has its own special energy. I see beauty in the patina of used materials that have been left behind through years of use and exposure. A scratch, a discolouration in the wood or a crinkle in the paper can give an object character and a sign of having lived.'

OPPOSITE:
Atlas, made from an old *Bosatlas*
(Dutch world atlas).

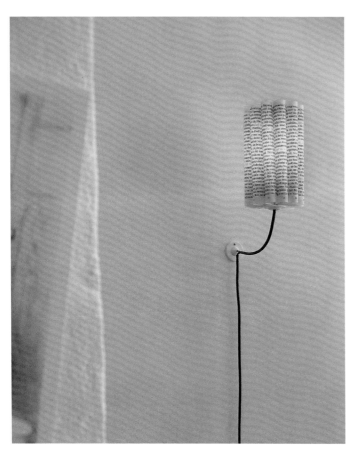

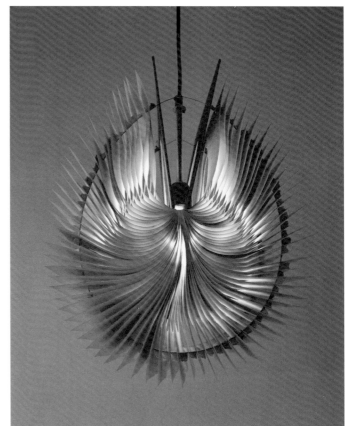

Moment 5, made from an old Dutch reading book.
All of the materials Bom uses have typographic
elements in them which he utilizes in an abstract
way to create graphic shapes.

Pegasus pendant lamp made from an old wine book.
Bom's work is about seeing the beauty of rejected
objects and finding ways to transform them into
functional sculptures. He conceives unique forms
from old books with the desire to create shapes that
are timeless and intriguing.

Globe, made from a *Reader's Digest* atlas from
the 1960s.

CLAIRE BREWSTER

London, United Kingdom

VINTAGE MAPS AND ATLASES > PAPER SCULPTURE

Lincolnshire-born Claire Brewster has been living and working in London for over 20 years. 'From the moment I learnt to pick up a pencil, art was the only thing I was really interested in,' she says. Whilst she was always working on her creative projects, her journey to becoming a professional artist involved living abroad in Spain and Romania as well as working for a high-profile architectural practice. Having pursued her art as a profession since 2000, she recently made the jump to work on her sculptures full-time.

It was artists such as Robert Rauschenberg, Kurt Schwitters and Joseph Cornell that first inspired Brewster to work with unconventional materials. Using old and out-of-date maps and atlases as her fabric, she cuts out intricate, delicate and detailed sculptures. 'My work is about retrieving the discarded, celebrating the unwanted and giving new life to the obsolete,' she says. Taking her inspiration from the natural environment, she creates entomological and ornithological installations of flora and fauna from imagined locations. 'My birds, insects and flowers transcend borders and pass freely between countries with scant regard for the rules of immigration or the effects of biodiversity. Nature is ever present, even in the most urban environments; it takes over anything we neglect,' she adds.

Most of the vintage maps used in Brewster's work are bought from eBay, though some are sourced from charity shops and flea markets. The process begins with making a drawing that is stuck to the back of the map before cutting. 'The print quality and the paper that was used in the 1920s and '30s is incredible. I cannot find the same quality in contemporary prints,' says Brewster. Sculptures are either pinned directly onto the wall for a large-scale installation or captured in box frames. When light is shone on the works, the shadows create a dynamic three-dimensional quality and a feeling of movement.

Brewster says, 'I love the idea of capturing insects in their moment of flight, a moment that is barely visible, something that we don't normally see. Monarch butterflies are amazing: they make a huge journey from North America to Mexico and their route is the same every year. In *On Our Way Home* (see pages 164–65) I wanted to highlight that this is some feat for such a small creature and a lot of the things that can go wrong on their journey are manmade.'

Often the bird breeds depicted correspond with the map's geographical location; at other times they can be perceived to be travelling to new lands. Brewster believes her work is about releasing the birds from the maps they are trapped in. Some of the titles of her works, such as *We Love This Place*, *It's Time to Get Out of Here* or *I Have Seen the Great Bear I Have*, are based on the imagined thoughts of the birds. She says, 'I always think they are trying to tell us something. They are annoyed with us because we have been given this beautiful earth and we don't take good care of it. The birds are fighting back.'

OPPOSITE:
Two bees from *A Crossing Bee*; *Africa Bee*; *Green Bee* triptych, 2012. Hand-cut pages from the *Oxford Advanced Atlas*, pins, foam board, box frame.

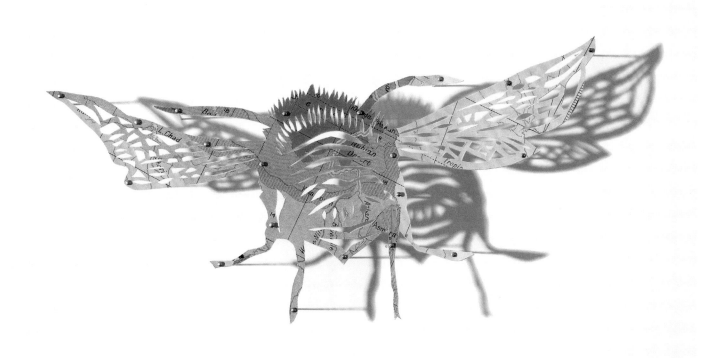

On a Secret Mission, 2013. Hand-cut RAF map of Scotland, pins, foam board, box frame. The number of parakeets spotted in Great Britain increased rapidly in the 1990s. Here, Brewster imagines they have left the warmth of their native land because they are on a secret mission.

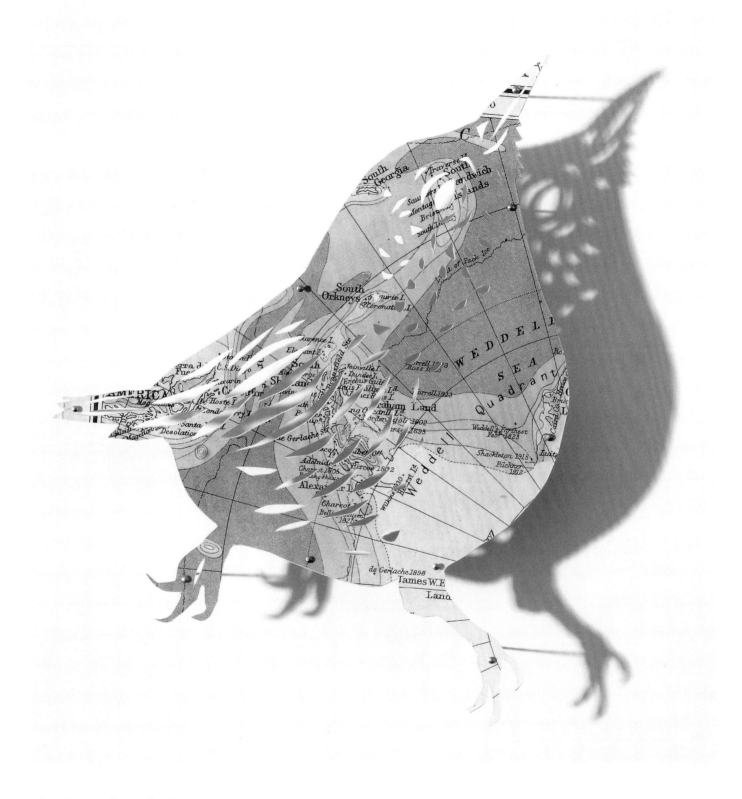

Blue Birdy, 2012. Hand-cut page from the
Oxford Advanced Atlas, pins, foam board,
box frame.

The Green Green Grass, 2012. Hand-cut map of London and the southeast of England, pins, foam board, box frame. This piece highlights the importance of nature as the city continues to encroach on the countryside.

ALVARO CATALÁN DE OCÓN

Madrid, Spain

USED PET BOTTLES > LIGHTING

After graduating with a degree in product design from Central Saint Martins, London, in 2004, two of Alvaro Catalán de Ocón's final-year projects went into production. After setting up his first studio in Barcelona, he moved to Madrid five years later, where he is now based. Catalán de Ocón and his team self-produce their designs, which allows them to oversee the entire design process from conception to completion. The design brief for the PET Lamp project began with the aim of spreading consciousness about the problem of plastic pollution in the Colombian Amazon River. He explains, 'We wanted to highlight the intrinsic contradiction that PET bottles are made to serve a purpose that lasts a matter of minutes, yet are made out of a material which takes centuries to disappear. We then thought of changing the use of the object by transforming it into a contemporary design with a strong visual impact. Realizing that the problem is global, we chose to combine this global industrial object with down-to-earth artisanal textile techniques and take the project to different countries all over the world.'

Catalán de Ocón began the project in collaboration with indigenous artisans from the Cauca region who had been displaced by the guerrilla war in Bogotá. 'We found that these communities had an ancestral knowledge which they couldn't put into practice. By allowing them to be part of the project, we could dignify their lives in Bogotá and learn from their amazing knowledge of weaving, particularly their use of patterns and colour. Their whole cosmogony began to appear in their work, which enriched the project exponentially,' he explains. As it was his first project using reclaimed materials, Catalán de Ocón had to adopt a very differ-ent working method. 'Used PET bottles are not always exactly the same, but I didn't want to find a solution that combined them with industrial processes. With something handmade you can expect a similar output but with small differences. The artisans also have the capacity to adapt to uneven materials.' After their first experience in Colombia, the team decided to try out the potential of the project by taking it to different cultures around the world. Their second workshop in Chile involved artisans who specialized in a wicker tradition, leading them to create larger, lighter lamps.

He says, 'It's hard to convince an artisan to combine a reclaimed material with their noble and traditional material. The big challenge is to have the reclaimed bottle seen and perceived as something which adds to the design rather than being regarded as a negative element. One of the great aspects of using the bottles in this way is how it allows each artist to improvise. It triggers the imagination of the artisan to reinvent their work every time they find a new bottle. A certain green might combine well with red and white or a red top would go well with a red line at the bottom. By showing artisans a method and leaving them the freedom to choose colours and patterns, we are able to offer a unique product to our customers. We can also serialize a unique object, and this is a very powerful tool that the industry can't offer you.'

He adds, 'The designer should be able to abstract the material in such a way that, even if it is seen or recognizable, it should enrich or bring humour to the final piece. The reuse of materials can't be the justification of the product but something which enriches the final result. The final object should defend itself.'

OPPOSITE:
Presentation of the PET Lamp Colombia at
Spazio Rossana Orlandi, Milan, 2013.

The first collection of Eperara-Siapidara
lampshades in Bogotá, 2013.

Eperara Siapidara artisan weaving a PET Lamp during the workshop in Bogotá, 2012.

Guambianos artisan Maria Estella Cuchillo cutting the PET bottle prior to weaving during the workshop in Bogotá, 2012. The manufacturing process of the bottle, which is made using moulds, always leaves two perfect vertical lines along the body of the bottle and a perfect horizontal line on the bottom. These elements allow artisans to cut the bottle precisely using simple tools.

Wicker fibre in the workshop of an artisan in Chimbarongo, Chile, 2014.

Raul Briones weaving a Triple PET Lamp Chimbarongo in his workshop in Chimbarongo, Chile.

OPPOSITE:

Presentation of the PET Lamp Chile at Spazio Rossana Orlandi, Milan, 2014.

JENNIFER COLLIER

Staffordshire, United Kingdom

DAMAGED BOOKS AND RECYCLED PAPER > PAPER SCULPTURE

Jennifer Collier completed a BA in textiles at Manchester Metropolitan University in 1999, specializing in print, knit and weave. Working from her studio, gallery and workshop space, Unit Twelve, in Stafford, West Midlands, she makes paper creations that put a contemporary twist on traditional textiles. Using paper sourced from damaged books in charity shops and flea markets, Collier uses the techniques of bonding, waxing, trapping and stitching to produce unusual paper fabrics. These are then used to make sculptures that are modelled on shoes, clothing and household objects.

'Towards the end of my course I started experimenting with different materials, weaving with orange peel, melting fruit bags: all manner of things my tutors did not approve of. I honestly believe that the best way to learn is by not being afraid to make mistakes; that way you allow yourself to have happy accidents. All of the techniques I now use in my work are things I have taught myself since graduating by experimenting with different media.'

She continues, 'I had started using heat-transfer printing to emulate the qualities of paper in my fabrics. It got to the stage where books and papers were my main inspiration, so it just made sense for them to become the media for the work. The paper also provides its own narrative. A dressmaking pattern becomes a sewing machine, for example, vintage photographs a camera, or the nursery rhyme 'Mary, Mary, Quite Contrary' a watering can. The

papers have their own history and their previous life fuels my ideas of what to create,' she explains.

Collier started using found and recycled materials around 15 years ago. Initially this was to save money on materials rather than being an ethical choice. 'Recycling wasn't the norm back then: we didn't have different bins for different types of rubbish. As time has gone on, however, this has become a very important niche to sit in, so much so that it is no longer a niche: people expect materials to be sourced responsibly.'

Each time a new piece is devised, Collier makes a pattern similar to the net of a box before producing a toile or maquette to check that the pattern or template works. She then creates a finished piece of work from beautiful found and recycled papers. Once she has perfected the pattern, she can apply it several times and will get quicker at making it each time. Detailed pieces such as *Paper Typewriter* (2012) can take up to a week to make because of all the different components.

She says, 'I love the fact that I am saving these beautiful but undervalued papers from landfill and adding value to items that others might overlook. I enjoy nothing more than finding a cookbook splattered with food stains or a water-damaged paperback that I can save from landfill and transform into something beautiful. Books that a child has loved enough to take the time to colour in the illustrations are an absolute treasure.'

OPPOSITE:
Jennifer Collier's studio space is based at Unit Twelve Gallery in Stafford. The studio is full of old maps and works in progress.

Paper Typewriter, 2012, made from vintage
typewriter manuals, grey board and machine
stitching.

Singer Sewing Machine, 2012, made from
dressmaking patterns and their instruction sheets,
grey board and machine stitching.

Paper Tea Set with Embroidered Tray, 2011, made from vintage wallpaper, letters, buttons, hand and machine stitching.

SARAH TURNER

Nottingham, United Kingdom

USED PLASTIC BOTTLES > LIGHTING

It was while working part time in Nottingham Trent University's coffee shop that artist and designer Sarah Turner began to realize how many plastic bottles are thrown away every day. She decided to start collecting them and experimented with various techniques to transform them. This eventually developed into a small lighting range that she exhibited at her graduate degree show. After graduating in furniture and product design in 2008, Turner set up her design business. As well as selling her lighting range in shops, galleries and online, her special commissions include a lighting scheme for Coca-Cola at the London 2012 Olympic Park and a custom-made sculpture which featured in an advertising campaign for SodaStream.

Organic shapes, curves and floral forms are a key feature of Turner's work. 'I enjoy the challenge of taking an item that is manmade and transforming it into something which looks like a natural object. I think people like to see that their rubbish is being used for something that's fun and good for the environment,' she says. Plastic bottles are collected from a network of donors made up of friends, family and strangers who are keen to help, a team Turner refers to as her 'bottle army'. As a result her garage, shed and conservatory at home are packed full of them. After a good clean the bottles are sandblasted, which turns the surface from transparent to frosted white. This allows her to dye the plastic bottles in vibrant colours. The bottles are then hand-cut with scissors and sculpted into beautiful, intricate forms.

Turner's early design influences include Ron Arad, Ryan Frank and Tord Boontje. She has also been inspired by frequent travels to Southeast Asia, where she witnesses a strong culture of recycling and make do and mend, in particular the resilience of the Thai people who had to rebuild their lives just months after the 2005 tsunami. She says, 'With any normal design process, you choose the material most suitable for the product you have designed. With upcycling you have to work around the material's limitations. The main challenge is making sure that the design is developed and refined. People don't want to buy something which appears home-made or looks as though they could make it themselves.'

OPPOSITE CLOCKWISE:

This large blue chandelier was built for the Ecobuild show at ExCel, London. Measuring 1.5 m wide, the light is made from 250 melted bottles.

Collected Coca-Cola bottles ready for sandblasting.

Chandelier (detail): 155 plastic bottles were hand-cut and sculpted into flowers that together formed a sphere 1 m in diameter. The piece was commissioned by Glendoick Garden Centre near Perth, Scotland.

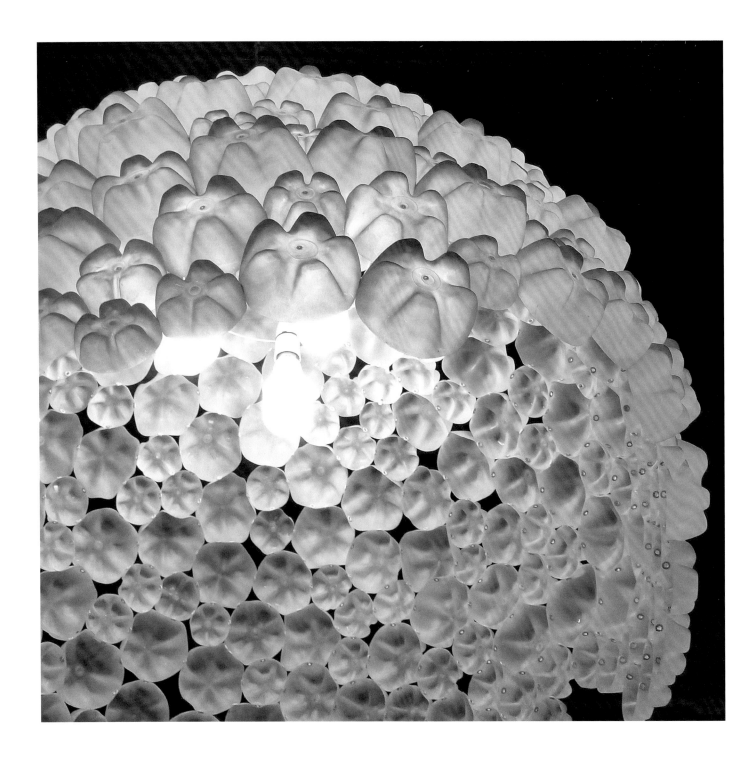

Ella is a large-scale ceiling pendant made from the
ends of different-sized plastic drinks bottles. It was
originally created for the Ideal Home Show, 2011.

Purple Cola 30, made from 30 locally collected
Coca-Cola bottles.

MEIKE HARDE

Saarbrücken, Germany

USED PLASTIC CUPS > LIGHTING

Meike Harde studied at the art school HBK Saar in the southwest German town of Saarbrücken. After getting her diploma in 2011 she did an internship at Studio Benjamin Hubert in London before returning to Saarbrücken to lecture at her university and open her own studio. Her eclectic range of projects is based on rethinking common manufacturing technologies.

Harde's project Lichtschlucker makes use of ice cream cups collected from ice cream sellers or disposable drinking cups picked up after parties. The cups have a good quality and density which means they can be used many times, despite usually being thrown away after one use. The Lichtschlucker project offered the disposable vessels a permanent life as a durable, functional and decorative lampshade. Cups were matched with those of the same type or mixed up with varying colours and forms. With the various angles, heights and widths of every cup, each had its own potential for a unique lamp shape. Harde tested each shape and turned the cups into lenses, bowls, cylinders and intricate molecular structures.

First and foremost, Harde's priority is to design products that are beautiful and intelligent. 'It is not always my primary intention to recycle materials but rather to design objects which are made with good-quality materials that result in long-lasting designs.' For the Lichtschlucker project, however, the use of reclaimed materials was motivated by a desire to find potential in something that would be thrown away. Seeing the cups as beautiful in their own right, she wanted to unveil their unique qualities when held up against light.

'A lot of my research on materials is done via the Internet. I really love the construction element in aesthetic work. Finding new ways to construct is a form of engineering. I like to work with special materials and techniques to find new applications,' says Harde. She believes that upcycling is important but that its reputation is not yet at its optimum level. 'It makes people more sensitive to the environment and can change their consumption habits, but a lot of bad upcycling still exists. In the future, it would be better if the waste in the upcycled product was no longer visible so that the products look more industrial and less self-made.'

OPPOSITE:

The Lichtschlucker project was about demonstrating the variety of shapes that can be made through the arrangement of simple drinking cups. Cups are tied to balls or ring-formations and are connected to create lenses, cylinders, bowl forms, molecule structures and free shapes. The neon cups are typical gelato cups from Italy.

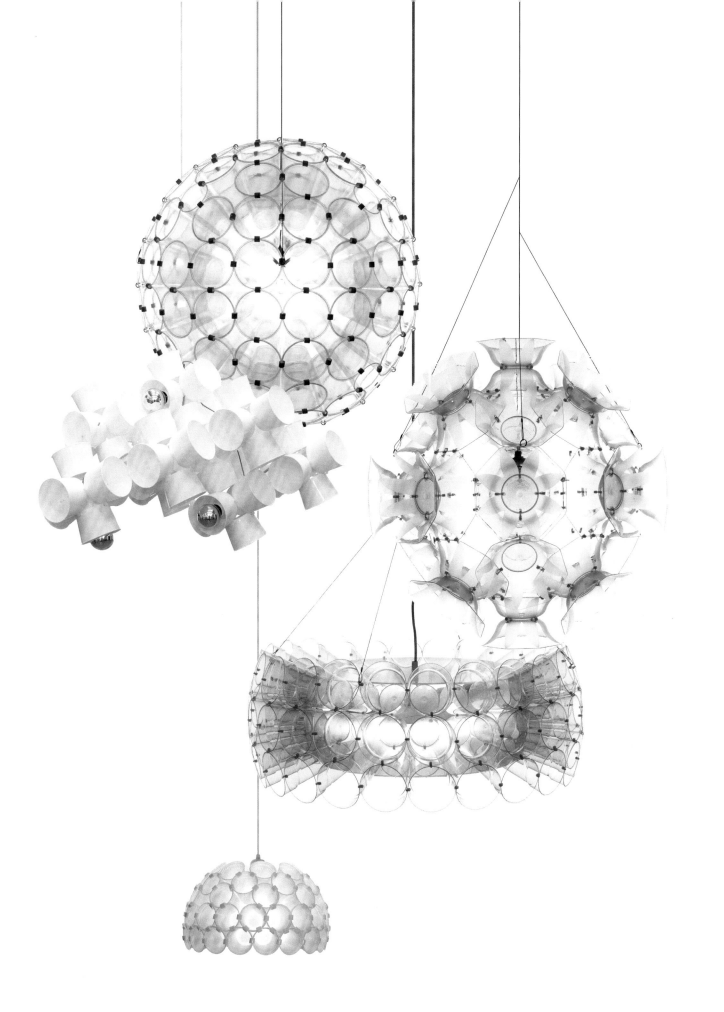

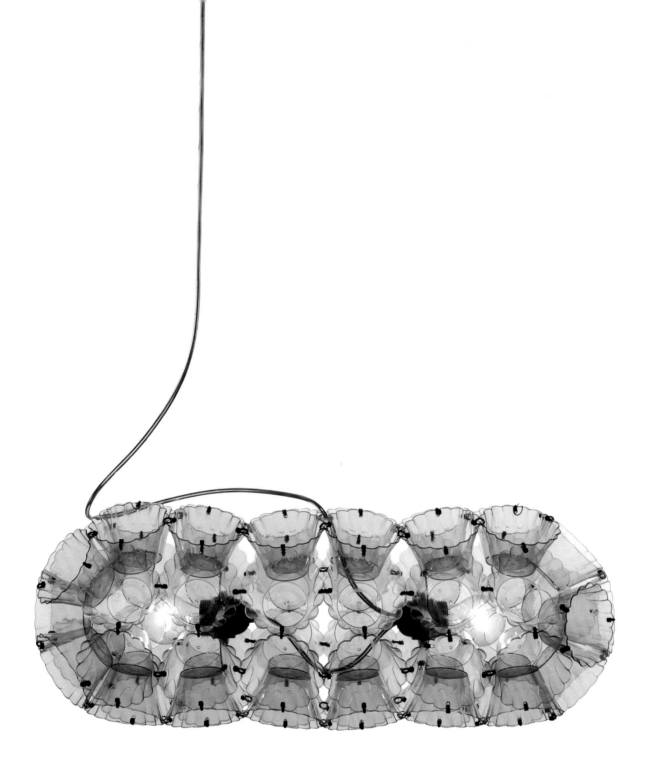

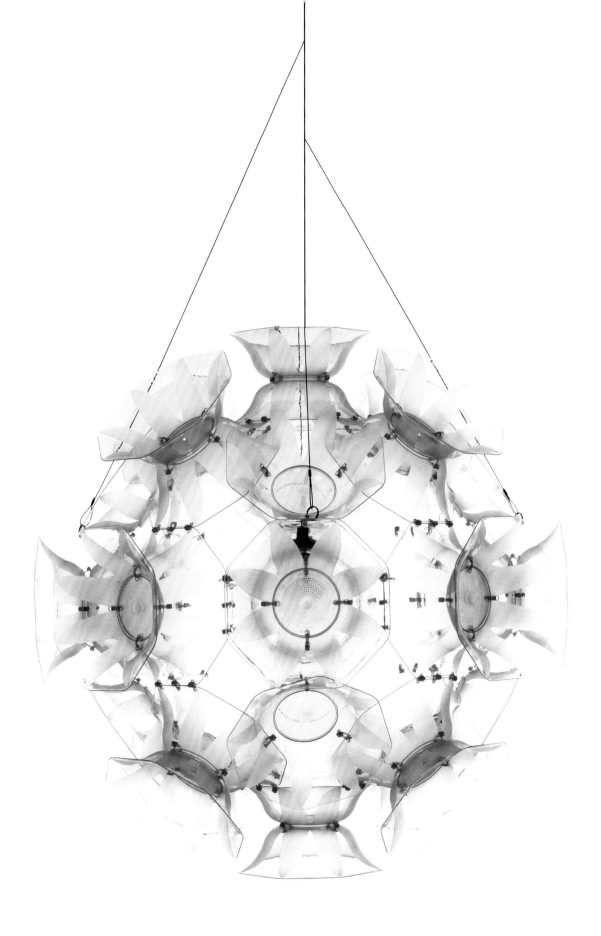

STEPHEN SOLLINS

New York, United States

Artist Stephen Sollins holds a BA in photography from Bard College and an MFA from the School of Visual Arts in New York. Galleries and museums that have held and exhibited his work include the Brooklyn Museum, the American Folk Art Museum, MoMA and the Fine Arts Museums of San Francisco.

Source materials have always been an important feature of Sollins's work and all carry domestic and sentimental associations. His chosen media include household linens, television schedules, camping supply catalogues and the daily newspaper. For Sollins, ideas and materials go hand-in-hand when generating a new body of work. 'Neither one can proceed without the other,' he says. 'I am interested in found materials partly because of an interest in the history of objects, but also because they have implications for the audience.'

In his *Piecework* series, Sollins combines the remains of two outmoded technologies, used mailing envelopes and traditional American quilt-making, in order to create large-scale works on paper. The works exemplify his ongoing interest in the integration of sentimentality with systems and rational structures. 'Sentimental handiwork and geometric precision are both present in traditional quilt-making patterns. These patterns reference homemaking, childhood, the bedroom and privacy, while embodying a geometric abstraction that pre-dated geometric abstraction,' explains Sollins. 'I am interested in using geometry, grids and the systematic approaches of high modern, minimal and conceptual art, in part to show how they do and do not relate to more popular and sentimental forms.'

The *Piecework* series is made from cut paper and Tyvek, a material often used for express mail envelopes. Materials are glued together using folded tabs, much like the sewn seams of a quilt. Sollins chose mailing envelopes as his medium because of their intersection between communication and privacy. Some of the envelopes used are saved from his own mail but he has also solicited donations from friends and family. Taking note of the patterns used to hide the contents, he noticed their surprising similarity to those found on vintage fabrics. He says, 'Their contents are banal yet guarded: private thoughts mingle with business records and utility bills. The bright colours and security tints of those envelopes, as they are gradually replaced by digital transactions, belie their guarded contents while evoking thoughts of a comforting domestic past.'

OPPOSITE:
Untitled (Double Archive with Rotation), 2013, from the *Piecework* series. Used envelopes (printed paper).

FOLLOWING SPREADS:
Untitled (Grandfather's Garden), 2013, from the *Piecework* series. Used envelopes (printed paper, Tyvek, acetate), with detail.

Untitled (Postscript), 2009, from the *Piecework* series. Used envelopes (printed paper, ink, pencil, acetate, foil).

Untitled (Afterthought), 2010, from the *Piecework* series. Used envelopes (printed paper, ink, pencil, acetate, stamps).

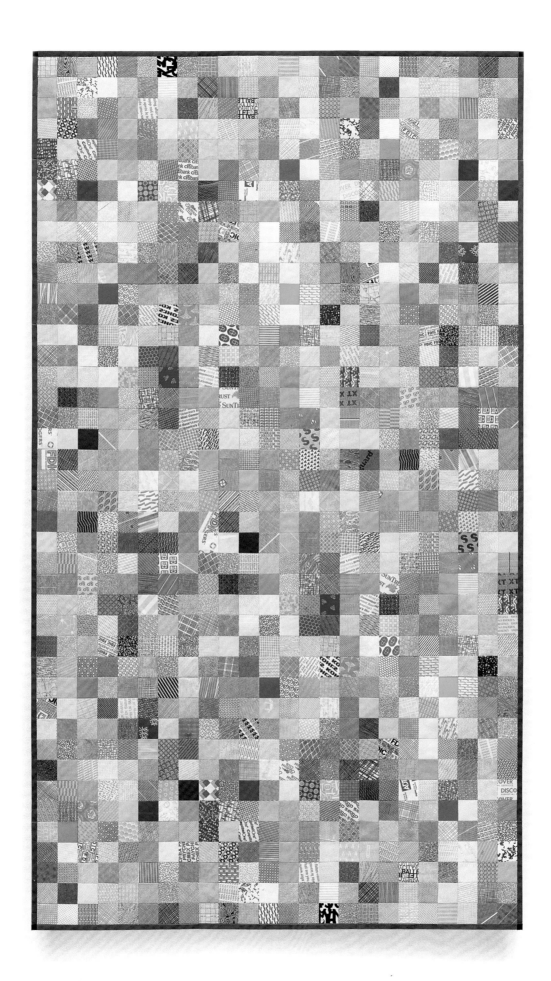

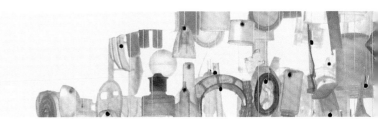
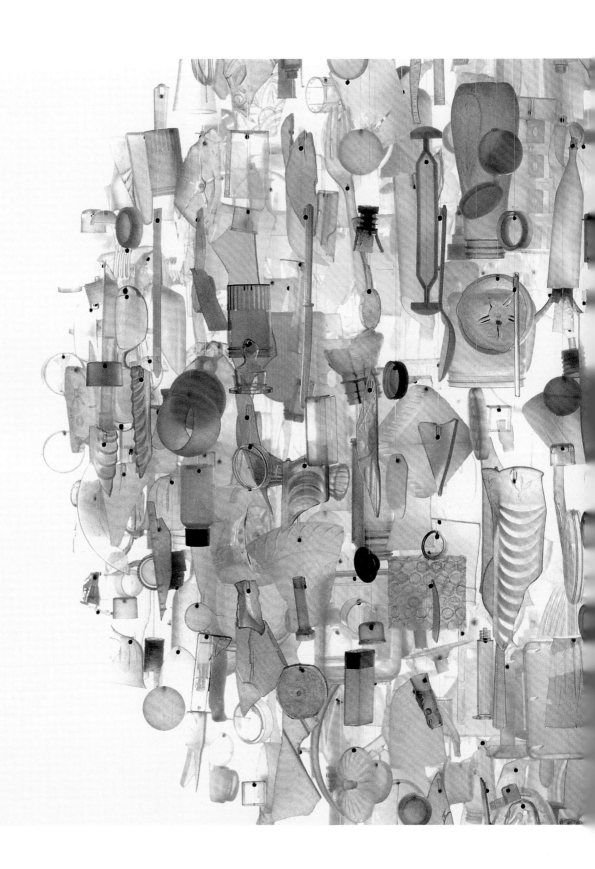

MIXED MEDIA

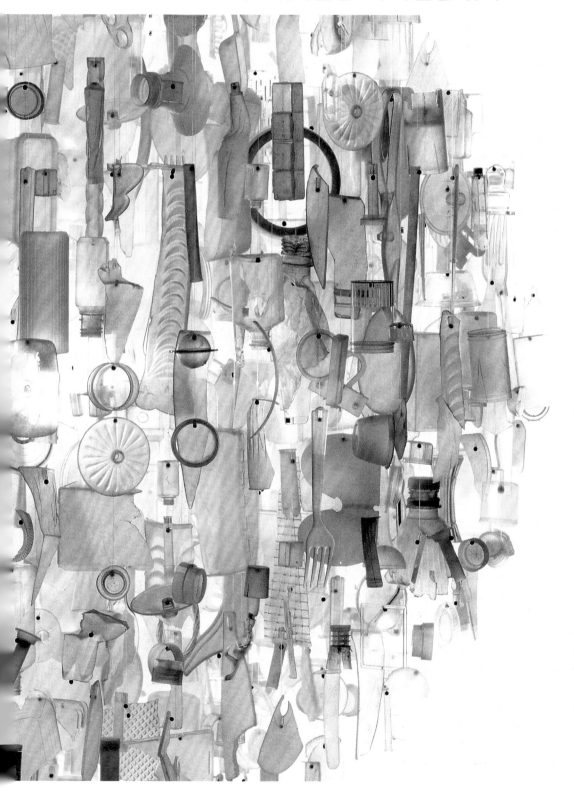

MADELEINE BOULESTEIX

London, United Kingdom

Prop maker Madeleine Boulesteix inherited the ability to create and construct from her architect father and dressmaker mother. The first chandelier she ever made was the result of a chance encounter with 40 faceted glass drops in a pile of rubbish. 'From humble objects I decided to create an opulent chandelier, a pastiche on luxury or the poor man's chandelier. When I started gathering other pieces that would enable me to form the structure, I discovered that all the things I needed were already there, just waiting for me to assemble them,' she says.

As a graduate in the late 1980s, reusing was a way of life and it was essential to pick up items at a bargain price. In the days when the term 'vintage' only applied to wine and cars, Boulesteix found all her second-hand components at her local scrapyard and at car boot sales. Now, searching anywhere from Paris flea markets to eBay, finding second-hand pieces cheaply has become harder and less predictable, with some items costing less in antique shops than in charity shops. 'The rise in demand for all things vintage has forced me to look harder for the discarded and unloved, but my work has always been about using something there isn't a demand for, so I continue to experiment with the less desirable components and find new ways to make them work. I look at the potential of an object, how it can be combined with something else to become something witty, beautiful and lasting. That is what keeps me entertained while I am working.'

Boulesteix describes her style as, 'very DIY, inventive, uncompromising and unfunded'. As a teenager, she was struck profoundly by the punk era, which still influences her work today. She says, 'The irreverence was so refreshing, like a folk art movement where a lot was done with very little at every level. An old kettle became a handbag, a big zip became a tie, a bunch of safety pins a brooch that was no less attractive than something from Asprey or more so. You made your own magazines with a photocopier. The depth to which the movement questioned value had a huge influence on me. As young punks we would wear old ladies' strappy sandals, zip-up ankle boots from charity shops, funny old hats from the 1950s and wrapover cotton housecoats. They were all considered ugly but they were actually really fabulous when worn with a bit of spirit.'

OPPOSITE:
Candlelit, 2011, made from teacups, baking moulds and other found ephemera.

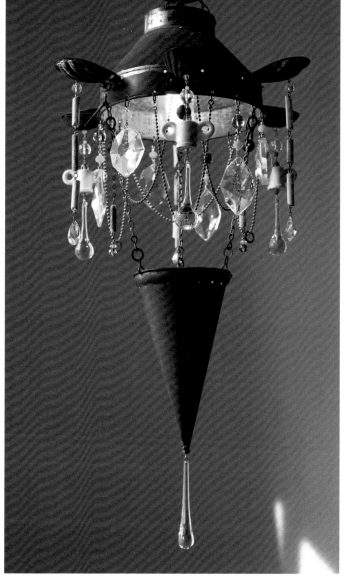

Carousel, 2011 (detail). Chandelier made with cupcake tins. To prevent the pinks from looking too sugary, they are offset with tarnished metal and rust.

Home Brew, 2013, made from two funnels, old clay pipe stems found on the Thames beach and old porcelain electric accessories from a Paris flea market. Boulesteix chose not to add any colour in order to let the hues and texture of the metal stand out.

A tray of croissant moulds bought from an antique trade market. Boulesteix has a policy of minimum intervention, meaning she introduces existing objects into her work without changing them so that they keep their character.

Sourcing materials at Walworth Road Market, South London.

ABOVE:
Madeleine Boulesteix in the studio with her
cat Otis.

OPPOSITE:
Mini Multi Fluted, 2011. A small jelly-bowl lantern.
Ideas for the chandelier's form come from the shape
and scale of the found objects. The design centres
around one dominant object before other objects
are added to it.

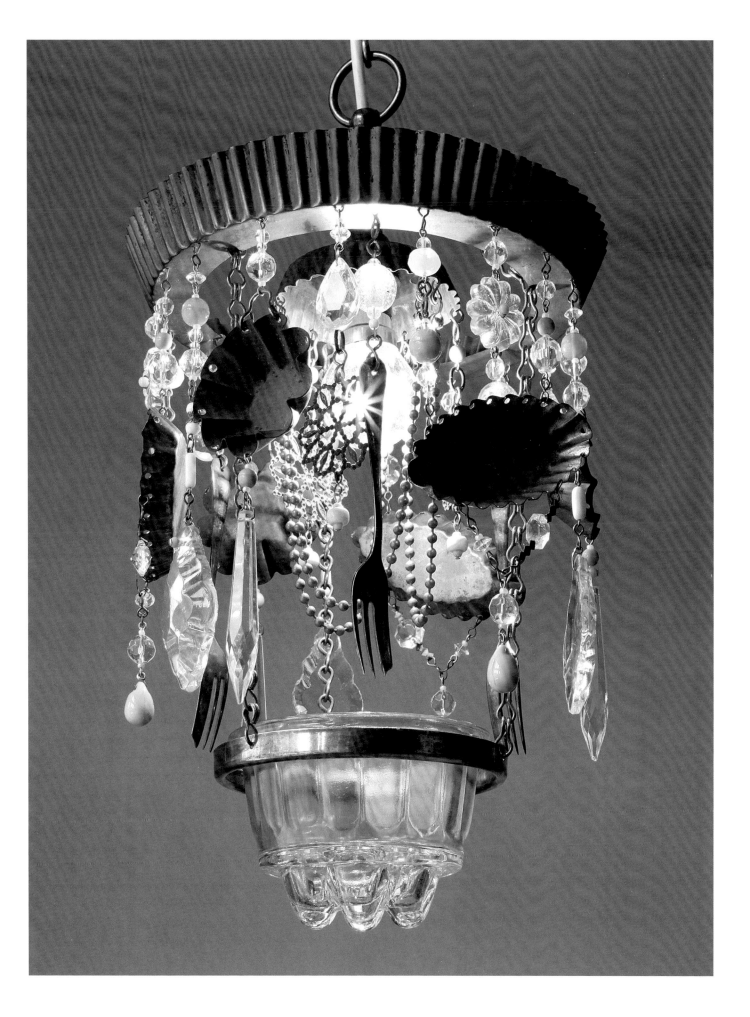

MANOTECA

Elisa Cavani | Bologna, Italy

FOUND FURNITURE AND OBJECTS > FURNITURE AND LIGHTING

After an education in design and communication, languages and architecture, Elisa Cavani dedicated 10 years to visual merchandising for fashion companies. In 2010 she decided to focus on her personal project Manoteca. With the help of retired craftsmen, she learnt various techniques that enabled her to create unique pieces out of carefully chosen objects from the past, transforming them for a new function.

'To me, collecting old abandoned objects and turning them into something new is a healthy creative process which allows me to change materials without damaging the environment,' says Cavani. 'The search for the right materials, however, can be a very long process. I am attracted to a shape, often without knowing what the object is, and I'll keep it with me until I find the right idea for it. Working with the objects is similar to writing a text. At the beginning it is just flow of consciousness and then I summarize and change it until everything is in balance.'

Cavani's works are not, however, assembled at random. Within each piece, every part of the composition has meaning. She says, 'Every hole, every flaw, every crack has a charm that a new object will never have: the colour of the wood oxidized by time, a soft and cosy shape, hardware that no longer exists. Owning an item made with recovered materials is owning a piece of someone else's life, a piece of history, as well as a piece of the life of the person who has reassembled it. I like the idea that the objects we choose are passed into the homes of other people. Some of the objects are three times my age and this fills me with great respect. If we are picking it up it is probably because it is still in good condition. The person who made it would perhaps be glad to know that the time dedicated to it was not in vain.'

Influenced by the ways in which the Surrealist painters expressed the unconscious through art, Cavani has always been inspired to search for a personal vision. 'I strive to look for an alternative to pre-packaged reality and rebel against attempts to have my work pigeonholed. The consumerist education leads us to choose the easiest way: buy a new one. It seems like an innocent act of convenience, because we can afford it, but it is in fact a dangerous process and anaesthetizes our minds when we should be finding alternative solutions such as improving the look of what we don't like anymore. Giving a second chance to something neglected pushes the boundaries, teaching us how to evaluate shapes and colours regardless of the original purpose of the object. It is about learning to see the world like a giant Lego city where anything can be mixed and become something else.'

OPPOSITE:

Indoor, made from doors sourced from the countryside near Modena, Italy, that were found on a pile of wood, waiting to be burned. When the doors are closed, Indoor is a dining table to seat 8 and when open, a desk with 3 inside pockets.

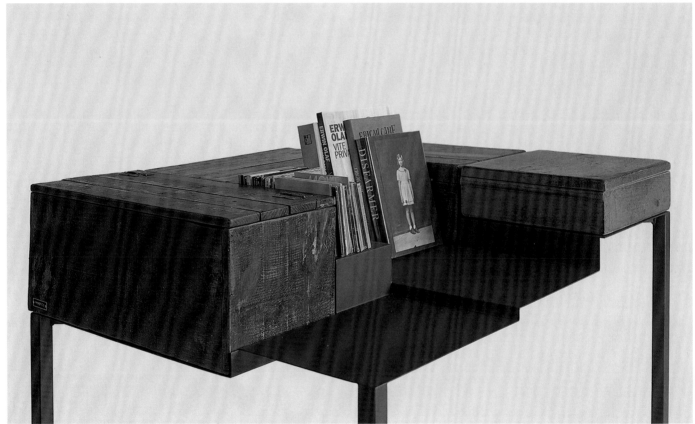

ABOVE:

Box Sir. All the boxes were made at the beginning
of the 20th century. They were also all irregular,
with no side equal to any another. To obtain
a perfectly flat tabletop, the frame had to be
carefully bent and also inclined.

OPPOSITE:

Ephemera. Cavani found this pharmacy desk in the
workshop of a restorer. One of the legs was broken
and many drawers were missing. Reborn as a ladies'
dressing table, the small, round mirror is a playful
addition that distorts the face instead of magnifying
it. 'It's a funny way to start the day,' says Cavani.

ABOVE AND OPPOSITE:
Il Fausto and Il Gino. Both of these tricycles were
found at a shop of antique toys. No longer able to
be used for the purpose they were built for, Cavani
thought they had a melancholic feel and decided
to give them a new life as lamps whilst respecting
their original function. The resulting forms have
a cartoon-character feel.

COUDAMY ARCHITECTURES

Paul Coudamy | Paris, France

From metal and chipboard to cardboard boxes, Paul Coudamy has always had a passion for optimizing materials, rich or poor. Since 2008 his practice has made architecture, interiors, furniture, lighting and installations that are visually unbounded, creating new processes on a daily basis. 'Our architectural and artisanal approach is due to the increasing demands from the residential and commercial market, both in terms of cost and aesthetics, but also for all things tailor-made,' says Coudamy.

For the F-Light project, created for the brand FLOWN Mobilier Airline, Coudamy's client offered them the possibility of creating a piece of design from old aeroplane parts. Made from an ultra-lightweight honeycomb composite material, the curved inner walls, windows and insulation of the Airbus A320 were cut away and reused to create luminous ceiling panels that resemble a levitating shell. Several of the light panels can be put together to fit rooms of any size.

Coudamy explains, 'These interior walls are marvels of engineering. Their ultra-functional curves are a result of uncompromising technical research yet would usually end up in landfill, left to rot. With F-Light, they are integrated back into our daily lives. We avoid having to use brand-new materials for a new product, but also offer redundant materials a second life.'

OPPOSITE AND OVERLEAF:

The windows of F-Light offer circles that diffuse the light across the whole surface of the panels. A second indirect lighting set on the structure reflects off the original silver insulation and enhances the feeling of levitation.

The curved inner walls and windows of F-Light create a dome that delineates the space and offers an intimate area beneath. Coudamy invented a structure that could be adapted to the shape of all planes. The panels can also be put together in a row to suit the desired dimensions.

SOPHIE CRICHTON

East Sussex, United Kingdom

FOUND FURNITURE, PLASTIC BAGS, COLLECTED OBJECTS > ILLUSTRATED FURNITURE

Sophie Crichton is a children's book illustrator with a love of making who regularly creates illustrations from imaginary worlds where animals talk and visit the hairdresser. The opportunity to paint humorous characters onto furniture has therefore added a new dimension to Crichton's artistic playground. Her introduction to creative reuse emerged when looking for a gift for her father. Finding an old abandoned chair on the pavement near her Kilburn flat, she painted the seat with a singing Mexican mariachi musician surrounded by cacti, smiling prawns, animal print and sunshine.

From then on, Crichton has applied her illustrations and passion for colour to a number of three-dimensional objects, transforming tired second-hand homeware into unique works of art. Whether perceived as furniture, sculpture or simply conversation pieces, Crichton is a firm believer that a chair doesn't have to be just a chair, but can bring an element of fun and humour to a space.

Influenced by the illustrations she creates for children, the designs on her furniture are often busy, with stimulating colours, objects and detail on every surface. 'I'm inspired by children's lack of fear and willingness to say whatever pops into their head at the time,' she says. This playful and uninhibited approach lends itself perfectly to the mixing up and reassembling of random objects, colours and characters that upcycling allows. Painting her illustrations three-dimensionally also enables her to animate furniture and other everyday items, simply by giving them ears, eyes, a nose and a mouth.

In addition to reviving tired pieces of furniture, she has developed other upcycling techniques through finding various tutorials online. Inspired by Mexican themes and colours, her Colores chair features a rush seat woven from 'plarn', a yarn made from used plastic carrier bags. Crichton says, 'While weaving, I lost my way about halfway through and I remember thinking "Shall I just undo it all?" But had it come out perfectly it may have looked machine-made. I think those imperfections are what gives it character.'

Crichton stresses the importance of surrounding ourselves with things that inspire us. 'So much of our personal information is shut away inside a computer. The things that lift our mood should be in view, to be enjoyed every day. I like it when a house says something about the person that lives in it. People come to my house and say "everything's got Sophie written all over it," but it's not a conscious thing.'

OPPOSITE:
La Tête Énorme. Crichton animates second-hand furniture with hand-painted illustrations. Using both acrylic and emulsion paints, a prior coating of white primer is the perfect base for her vibrant colour palette.

ABOVE:

Showtime was an old chair picked up at the
YMCA. Crichton painted and adorned the chair
with random collected objects such as beer labels,
bottle tops, buttons, tickets, glitter, bits of string
and even foreign currency. Made for a friend, the
seat reads 'Caroline Belongs to This Chair'.

OPPOSITE:

Padre chair. Every surface of the chair was hand-
painted in a different colour or pattern. Pockets of
colour reveal surprising humorous details that can
only be seen on closer inspection.

Painted boxes, originally IKEA drawers. Crichton's
illustrations combine her French heritage with a
love of warm Mexican colours.

Colores chair. Bought from the YMCA, the chair's
broken seat was removed in order to be replaced
with a new rush seat which Crichton made from
woven 'plarn', a yarn made from recycled plastic
carrier bags.

KIRSTEN HASSENFELD

New York, United States

FOUND OBJECTS, VINTAGE GIFT WRAP, USED PAPER > SCULPTURE AND INSTALLATION

Exhibited extensively in the United States at venues such as the Brooklyn Museum, MoMA PS1 and the Jewish Museum in New York as well as abroad, Kirsten Hassenfeld's sculptural paper and assemblage works are renowned for their innovative use of materials and intricate construction. Her fantasy structures and environments evoke a world of plentitude and fragility. Influenced by interpretations of nature in the decorative arts of the 18th and 19th centuries, her objects explore notions of wealth and status. By borrowing elements from jewellery, interior decor, architecture, mineralogical formations and botanical patterns, she has for the last decade focused on interpreting familiar precious forms and elements from the natural realm, utilizing used paper and materials recycled from her daily life.

Reclaimed objects first entered Hassenfeld's work in the piece *Pixie Mix* (2010), when she was asked to create a permanent public artwork in a school. In search of a material that was more durable than translucent papers and that could withstand the site, she decided to use the longevity and stability of unwanted materials to her advantage. 'My logic was that nothing seems to endure more than junk. It was also very satisfying not to rely on conventional art materials. It presented an extra challenge, but gave me a rich source of inspiration. Many of the objects were recognizable and

that gave the work an exciting dimension for the children who were the primary viewers.'

Avoiding adding to the demand for new materials is an extension of environmentally aware practices from Hassenfeld's everyday life. She says, 'When something breaks in my house, I check it for possible elements I could use before discarding it. A broken toy car might yield a few interesting plastic parts, for example.' In recent years, paper works such as *Cabin Fever* (2012) and *Star Upon Star* (2011) have also been constructed from used and vintage gift-wrap harvested from donations, eBay and yard sales. She also reuses the insides of security envelopes that she saves from bills.

Hassenfeld explains, 'I am fascinated by the two extremes: lavish decorative objects made of precious materials but with no real use, and functional objects that are also beautiful and made from trash. Referencing forms found in nature and luxury goods, my structures are suffused with complex relationships as patterns and images overlap and interact. Histories and traditions become jumbled together with everyday consumerism. In my earlier work, the materials I used were blank or mostly neutral. I now enjoy the challenge of turning varied materials, some ugly, some beautiful, into something new.'

OPPOSITE:

Pixie Mix, 2010, made from found glass, metal, ceramic, plastic, wood, shell, enamel. Hassenfeld was asked to build a hanging work for the vestibule of the new early childhood centre of an elementary school. In searching for a durable material that would withstand the rigours of the site, she decided to use only materials she could find discarded or in thrift stores.

Star Upon Star, 2011, made from recycled gift wrap with mixed media and, behind, *Blue Star*, made from recycled gift wrap and envelopes with mixed media (exhibition view from *American Dreamers*, Centre of Contemporary Culture, Palazzo Strozzi, Florence). Both pieces are constructed spikes made with five- and six-sided bases, assembled to form a truncated icosahedron, the same form associated with a football. The skeleton is constructed from hand-rolled paper tubes connected by pipe cleaners.

Cabin Fever, 2012. Made from recycled gift wrap and envelopes with mixed media, this work was conceived for the ground-floor exhibition space of the Hunterdon Art Museum in Clinton, New Jersey, which was formerly a stone mill. Hassenfeld took inspiration from the site and investigated the vernacular handicrafts of the pioneers during the westward expansion in America.

Treen Three, 2011, installed at the Albany International Airport, Albany, New York. Made from found glass, metal, ceramic, plastic, wood, shell, enamel, cardboard.

Treen Three, 2011 (detail). For her *Treen* series, Hassenfeld creates stacks of everyday objects such as jar lids, bottle caps, discarded kitchenware and buttons sourced from thrift stores, rummage sales and friends. Questioning notions of value, the resulting forms resemble turned decorative ivory and wood, popular with 18th-century European nobility.

STUART HAYGARTH

London, United Kingdom

COLLECTED FOUND OBJECTS > LIGHTING AND INSTALLATION

Previously working in graphic design and photography, Stuart Haygarth has been working as an artist and designer since 2004. His chandeliers, installations and sculptures revolve around large collections of objects that take on new meaning through the way in which they are assembled, giving new significance to the seemingly banal.

Objects used in Haygarth's work range from prescription spectacle lenses to smashed wing mirrors, vehicle light lenses and disposable plastic wine glasses. Using light, and alternative methods of presentation, he turns objects from the ordinary to the luxurious. The works are made and sold as limited editions of around 10 pieces. Each individual piece is unique but is created using the same types of found objects to the same formula. One of Haygarth's early inspirations is the Dutch design company Droog, who were renowned for working with found and industrial materials in the 1990s. His work is also about the power of collections and archives, methods which by their very nature create a sense of preciousness and intrigue around objects.

The process begins with collecting objects of interest. Items are sourced from various locations, including the streets of London, flea markets, car boot sales, charity shops, eBay and beaches all over Europe. He says, 'With most of the found objects, there is a period of taxonomy, intense cleaning and slight modification. The items sometimes remain in my studio for months or even years. I simultaneously work on possible ideas in my sketchbook, which are also left to ferment for lengthy periods. I return to the ideas over and over and if they still interest me, I'll decide to develop them further. The period of gestation and re-engaging with objects and their potential is akin to a prolonged process of testing. I test whether the ideas hold weight and interest, whether they fire my imagination and continue to feel pertinent. If that is the case I will spend time collecting the objects in greater numbers until I have enough to fulfil the project.'

He adds, 'Because reclaimed or found objects have a history, they take on a personality that new objects don't have. The plastic ephemera collected on beaches which are incorporated into my work *Tide* (2004), for example, have been distressed over a long period by the sand and seawater. Their shape has been transformed and the colours faded by the salt and air. All the objects have been through a process which cannot be truly replicated. I think the most successful of my works operate best when the objects are not immediately recognizable, but on closer inspection the viewer is surprised to notice what the work is composed of. I like to use everyday objects so that most people can quickly relate to them in some way and then see them transformed in a new context.'

OPPOSITE:

Raft – Dogs, 2009, made from collected ceramic dog figurines. Haygarth made a similar lampshade, *Raft – Cats*, in 2009, from collected ceramic cat figurines. The two collections explore why cats and dogs have become the most popular and widespread of domestic creatures, to the point where humans are defined by being either a cat person or a dog person.

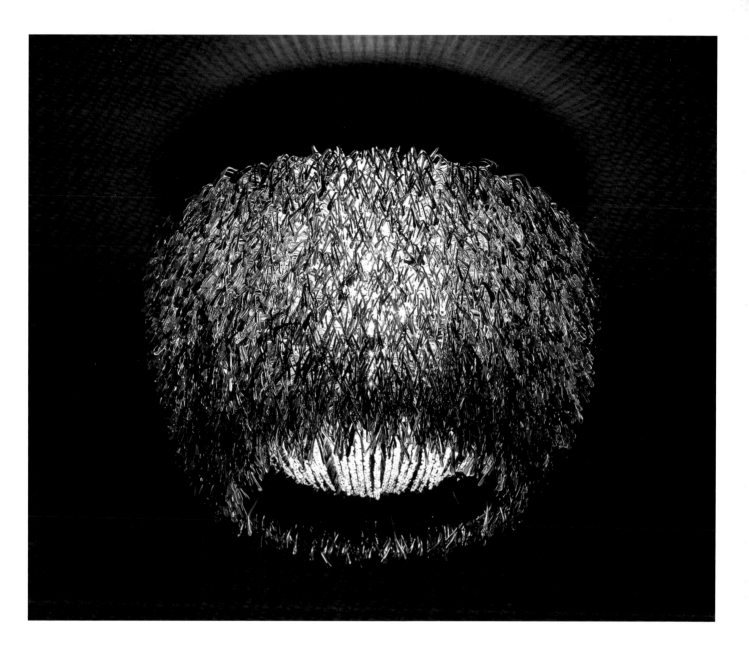

OPPOSITE:
Tide, 2011, installed at The Collection Museum, Lincoln, UK. The original *Tide* chandelier was part of a larger body of work based on the collection of manmade debris found on a specific stretch of the Kent coastline. The chandelier is created from clear and translucent objects, primarily made of plastic. Each object is different in shape and form, yet they come together to produce a perfect sphere 1 m in diameter. The sphere is an analogy for the moon, which affects the tides and in turn washes up debris. The objects hang on monofilament line held from an MDF platform above (see also pages 202–03).

ABOVE:
Urchin, 2009, is created from thousands of selected spectacle arms which are linked together to produce three individual forms. Installed flush to the ceiling, they have a shaggy, organic appearance resembling sea urchins or stalactites growing from an underground cave. They are illuminated from within by a stamen containing ribbons of LED lights.

Spectacle, 2006, detail of chandelier made from over
1,000 used pairs of prescription, plastic-framed
spectacles, which, through being linked together,
resemble a tiered chandelier.

Optical Chandelier, 2009, made from over 4,500
tinted prescription spectacle lenses hung on
monofilament line from a platform. The spherical
shape imitates a disco ball; the light is refracted
rather than reflected through the many layers of
glass lenses, resulting in a magical explosion of light.

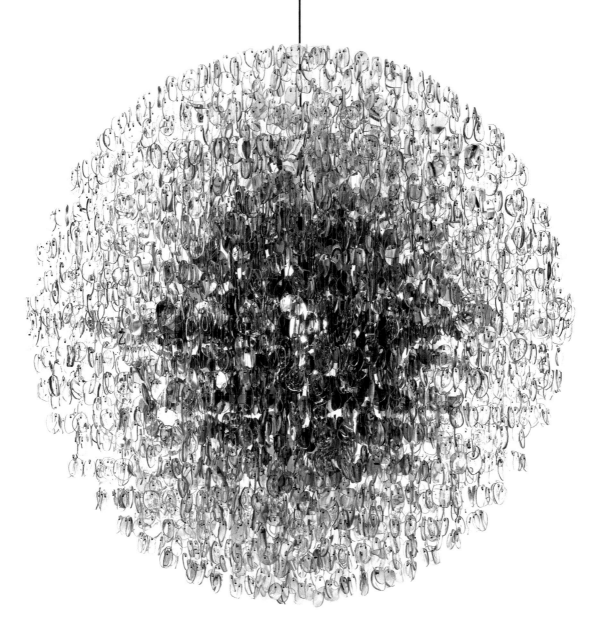

MICHAEL JOHANSSON

Malmö, Sweden, and Berlin, Germany

FOUND FURNITURE AND OBJECTS > INSTALLATION

After studying at the Trondheim Academy of Fine Art in Norway, and Kunsthochschule Berlin-Weissensee in Germany, Michael Johansson took his masters degree at Malmö Art Academy, Sweden, in 2005. Currently living and working between Malmö and Berlin as a full-time visual artist, Johansson has taken part in several residencies and frequently exhibits his work internationally. Resembling life-size Tetris building blocks, his sculptures and installations are comprised of tightly stacked ordinary objects that are assembled into streamlined shapes in unexpected spaces, often grouped together by colour.

Johansson has always been a collector, but was fortunate enough to realize early on that collecting comes with limitations. He says, 'If one wants to tell a story with objects like I do, that story needs a beginning and an end: a defined space. Being a hoarder is something completely different. What intrigued me to create these works was the duality of the potential chaos in combination with all the necessary limitations in colours, themes and volumes. I wanted to create a physical manifestation of a perfect system.'

Johansson's work is about forming coherence between space and material. In some cases the spaces dictate the work; at other times the objects do. Ideas for new work, however, can also come before finding either. He finds most of the objects in flea markets and second-hand stores in the area where he lives but, if working on a project abroad, he will usually spend some time collecting things he can use on site beforehand. For his series of site-specific works within museums or galleries, many objects are borrowed from the storage spaces of the institutions for the duration of the exhibitions.

Johansson says, 'Everyday scenarios inspire me tremendously. I have always enjoyed spotting all kinds of irregularities or patterns in my surroundings. The same rule applies to my art practice. There has to be a combination of the highly recognizable with the unique in order to create a fruitful encounter between the work and the viewer. Underlying all these ordinary objects that most people can recognize from daily life are subjects for wider discussion such as history, memory and tangibility. One contemporary dialogue my work might trigger is our need to discuss our massive surplus of things. Since each work contains hundreds of different objects, all found in different places, it is as though many lives become morphed together into a fake identity that never existed.'

OPPOSITE:

Tetris, 2014. Permanent public installation in the library at Bok and Blueshus, Notodden, Norway. Most of the items were found at local second-hand stores or were outdated items salvaged from the former library. Notodden has a strong connection to blues music and hosts a famous blues festival every year, so Johansson wanted the work to be connected to music in some way.

Shade, 2013. Ordinary items installed at Galleri Andersson/
Sandström, Stockholm, Sweden. The installation formed part of
Johansson's solo exhibition. Working on such a large scale, one of
the challenges was producing a supportive structure that could
hold the weight of all the smaller items and harmonize with the
gradual change in colour running through the work. Putting all
the pieces together on site took approximately 10 days.

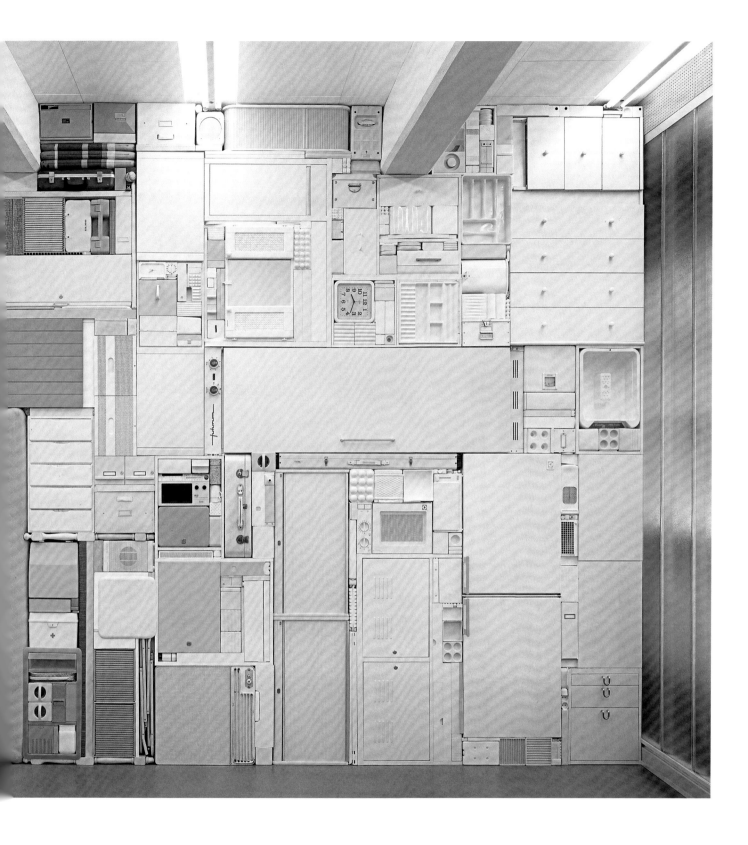

SWARM

Leslie Oschmann | Amsterdam, Netherlands

VINTAGE OIL PAINTINGS, FOUND FURNITURE AND OBJECTS > FUNCTIONAL ART

Leslie Oschmann's passion for making goes back to childhood, when she assisted her dad with his carpentry business. Since the late 1990s, Oschmann has worked as a manager and buyer for Conran and Habitat as well as taking the role of visual director at branches of Anthropologie across the United States. After leaving her career in retail merchandising in 2006, she has come full circle and honed a childhood passion into a lifestyle. She now creates objects under her own label Swarm from her Amsterdam studio.

'Since I moved to Europe, I have been a collector of materials from old markets in Brussels, Lille, Utrecht, Ghent, Bruges and Amsterdam. It was a natural transition for me to search for items that I can manipulate, recreate and bring new life to. I have always been compelled by the beauty of objects. Whether it's old oil paintings, vintage silk scarves, quirky bedside tables, old textile samplers or Belgian bank bags, I catalogue these finds in my studio and draw upon them when I begin working,' says Oschmann.

From furniture to wall decor, the pieces Oschmann creates vary greatly in size, colour and style, but there is one common thread. Each is thoughtfully manipulated and intended to inspire the eye in a clever and unexpected manner. Some of the most interesting examples can be found in her reuse of vintage oil paintings by unknown artists. Sourced from markets, many of the paintings are damaged and timeworn. The canvas is used as a material to make bags, chair coverings, stationery and even artificial flowers. 'I have been able to make multiple contacts for collecting paintings. They derive from a highly funded arts programme in Belgium and the Netherlands from years ago, now on the decline. There is an amazingly large quantity of them out there,' she says.

Oschmann has also experimented with textile techniques. For her piece Weaving Chair – Danish II she gives renewed energy and design appeal to found chairs using a macramé and weaving technique from the 1970s. The weaving is applied asymmetrically with contrasting colours. 'The final result is a modern update on a traditional sensibility that stands alone as a chair or a piece of art, or both,' she says.

Inspired by the sense of whimsy in Dutch design, in particular the work of Jurgen Bey, Oschmann's attraction to reclaimed items started while she was working in visual merchandising. She says, 'Working to a budget meant having to be thrifty. It was a good challenge. Something worn is also more in line with my aesthetic. I am inspired by materials both new and old.'

OPPOSITE:
Oschmann turns unwanted vintage paintings into decorative details on furniture. Here, the frames are integrated into a pair of found chairs.

OPPOSITE:
Painting Chair – Still-life. Time-worn painted
canvases repurposed on to a vintage chair.

ABOVE:
Weaving Chairs – Danish II and Thonet II.
Vintage chairs are embellished with macramé-
inspired weaving techniques from the 1970s.

Painting Bag – Dachshund. Oschmann has made a
series of leather handled tote bags from vintage oil
paintings sourced exclusively from Holland
and Belgium.

JONAS' DESIGN

Jonas Merian | Shanghai, China

For 17 years, Swiss-born Jonas Merian worked in prosthetics and orthotics in Switzerland, North Korea and China. Through his education and experience as a prosthetist he learned to work with a wide variety of materials, such as wood, leather, metal, resin, silicone, carbon fibre, textiles and plastics. In 2009 he took a break from his career to concentrate on furniture design. A year later, Merian and his partner renovated an old Shanghai factory building into a loft and design studio.

Merian's projects are focused on using reclaimed materials and objects from Shanghai's past, particularly old Chinese furniture and reclaimed wood from the destroyed Old Town. His preferred materials to work with, however, are the everyday objects that he finds at local antique markets and thrift stores, which Merian believes carry an aesthetic that is impossible to replicate. Through his creations he strives to keep part of Shanghai's increasingly disappearing history alive.

Merian initially used reclaimed materials as a way of saving money. He says, 'When we renovated our loft, we needed furniture for our big studio, so I started to make pieces from anything I could find. I always liked the aesthetics of antiques that are well worn and show the traces of time. After making the first furniture pieces, I fell in love with it and found I had many more ideas.'

Merian's portfolio now boasts every kind of reuse project imaginable. As well as his heavy wooden Long Tang tables, he makes cabinets from old suitcases, lamps from beer bottles, clocks from telephones, speakers from biscuit boxes and digital picture frames from old 1960s televisions, all of which he has used to furnish his loft apartment.

As Merian is a self-taught carpenter, he has not only found the upcycling process helpful in learning new skills: it has enabled him do something creative with pieces that are beyond his skill set, such as making bathroom furniture with objects that boast intricate woodcarvings. He says, 'I like the process of going out and exploring new places to find nice materials. It's time-consuming but rewarding once you find a nice piece. The wood often looks ugly at first but as soon as you remove the first few layers, it turns into a beautiful material. You sometimes can't tell that it's old wood. In China, the concept of upcycling is very new and not many people understand it. It is mainly Chinese people who were exposed to upcycling whilst growing up or studying abroad that buy my products. My biggest market is foreigners living in China. Although upcycling is not yet as big in the East as it is in the West, I expect this to change very soon. I think it is a movement that will accompany us into the future as more people make eco-conscious purchases.'

OPPOSITE:
Kettle table lamp made from a typical aluminium Chinese kettle mounted on reclaimed wood with an adjustable goose neck.

ABOVE:

Merian has furnished his loft apartment with his
own upcycled pieces and vintage finds. This wall
cabinet is made from a repurposed suitcase, the
clock from a vintage telephone and a letter box
from a PET water dispenser.

OPPOSITE CLOCKWISE:

Clocks made from old Chinese biscuit tins from the
1970s and '80s.

Clock made from a vintage telephone.

Merian's loft in Shanghai. Much of the renovation
was done using second-hand bricks and reclaimed
wood from demolished houses. The moveable
gas stove and kitchen table are made from old
Chinese tables covered with stainless steel. Over the
reclaimed wood Long Tang table 2.0 hangs a Triple
Kettle lamp, an adjustable light made from a piece
of water pipe and repurposed aluminium kettles. A
Chinese biscuit tin filled with concrete is used as a
counterweight.

Lamp made from an old Chinese biscuit tin.
The lamp can be dimmed or switched on and off
by touching the tin anywhere.

OPPOSITE:

Metal cabinet made of varnished rusty steel and
reclaimed wood.

Shelf made from old Chinese biscuit tins and
reclaimed wood. Images on the vintage tins range
from kittens and goldfish to romantic Western
couples playing golf.

DIRECTORY

+BRAUER
brauer.fr
brauergalerie.com

ATELIER BOMDESIGN
bomdesign.nl

ATTENDANT CAFÉ
the-attendant.com

BEAT UP CREATIONS
beatupcreations.com

BLEU NATURE
bleunature.com/en

BOKJA DESIGN
bokjadesign.com

JULI BOLAÑOS-DURMAN
julibd.com

BON RESTAURANT
corvincristian.com/en
bonrestaurant.ro

MADELEINE BOULESTEIX
madeleineboulesteix.co.uk

CLAIRE BREWSTER
clairebrewster.com

BRUT CAKE
brutcake.com

ALVARO CATALÁN DE OCÓN
catalandeocon.com
petlamp.org

JENNIFER COLLIER
jennifercollier.co.uk

COUDAMY ARCHITECTURES
coudamyarchitectures.com/en

SOPHIE CRICHTON
sophieillustration.co.uk

ESTHER DERKX
estherx.nl

DVELAS
dvelas.com

FACARO
facaro.com

FUN MAKES GOOD
funmakesgood.co.uk

YELI GU
guyeli.com

MEIKE HARDE
meikeharde.com

KIRSTEN HASSENFELD
kirstenhassenfeld.com

STUART HAYGARTH
stuarthaygarth.com

WILLEM HEEFFER
willemheeffer.com

HENDZEL + HUNT
hendzelandhunt.com

HÖST RESTAURANT
cofoco.dk/da/restauranter/hoest
newnorm.dk
normcph.com

MICHAEL JOHANSSON
michaeljohansson.com

JONAS' DESIGN
jonasdesign.net

LES M&MDESIGNERS
behance.net/martinleveque
behance.net/math_ology

MANOTECA
manoteca.com

EL NEBOT DEL PERSIANER
elnebotdelpersianer.com

NIC PARNELL
nicparnell.com

RAFINESSE & TRISTESSE
rafinesse-tristesse.com

THE RAG AND BONE MAN
theragandboneman.co.uk

ALEX RANDALL DESIGN
alexrandall.co.uk

MEB RURE
meb-rure.com

STEPHEN SOLLINS
stephensollins.com

MARKUS FRIEDRICH STAAB
markusfriedrichstaab.com

STUDIO BRIEDITIS & EVANS
reragrug.blogspot.se
brieditis.se
broderievans.blogspot.se

SWARM
swarmhome.com

TING LONDON
tinglondon.com

SARAH TURNER
sarahturner.co.uk

CAROLA VAN DYKE
carolavandyke.co.uk

WINDOW HOUSE
lilahhorwitz.com
oldworldgrange.tumblr.com

YESTERDAY RECLAIMED
yesterdayreclaimed.com

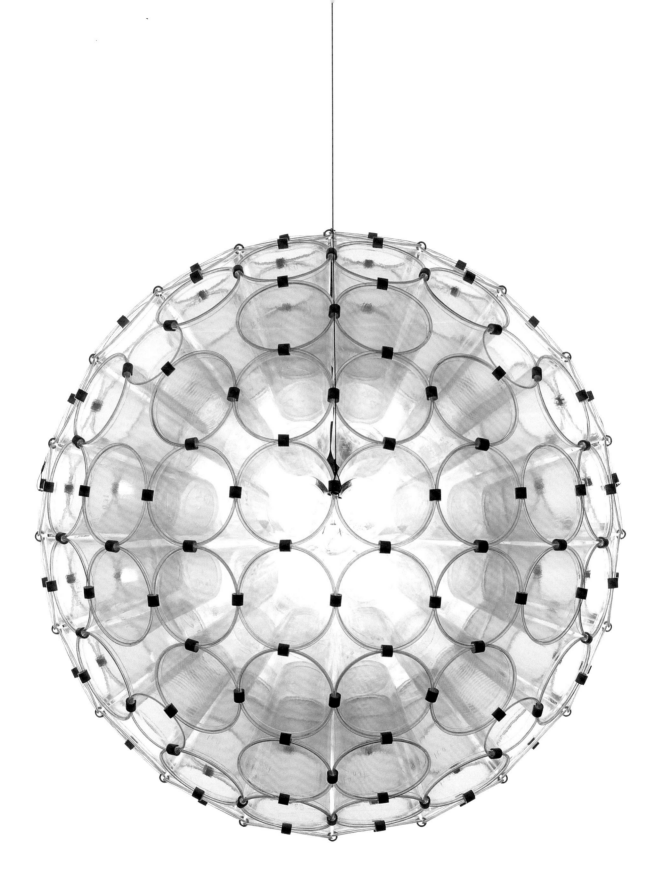

for John Brooke Edwards

ACKNOWLEDGEMENTS

A huge thank you to all the designers, artists, makers and photographers who contributed to *Upcyclist*.

Special thanks go to Ali Gitlow, Andrew Hansen, Martha Jay and Prestel Publishing. Thanks especially to Paul Sloman for his collaboration, invaluable help and advice.

Thanks also to the following for all your encouragement and support: Sophie Crichton, Georgios Kopanias, Jacqueline Milborrow, David Milborrow, David Neal, Elizabeth Simpson.

PICTURE CREDITS

© Prestel Verlag, Munich · London · New York, 2015
© for the text by Antonia Edwards, 2015
© for the images see Picture Credits, p. 255, 2015

Prestel Verlag, Munich
A member of Verlagsgruppe Random House GmbH

Prestel Verlag
Neumarkter Strasse 28
81673 Munich
Tel. +49 (0)89 4136-0
Fax +49 (0)89 4136-2335

www.prestel.de

Prestel Publishing Ltd.
14–17 Wells Street
London W1T 3PD
Tel. +44 (0)20 7323-5004
Fax +44 (0)20 7323-0271

Prestel Publishing
900 Broadway, Suite 603
New York, NY 10003
Tel. +1 (212) 995-2720
Fax +1 (212) 995-2733

www.prestel.com

Library of Congress Control Number: 2014952950

British Library Cataloguing-in-Publication Data: a catalogue record for this book is available from the British
Library; Deutsche Nationalbibliothek holds a record of this publication in the Deutsche Nationalbibliografie;
detailed bibliographical data can be found under: http://dnb.d-nb.de

Prestel books are available worldwide. Please contact your nearest bookseller or one of the above addresses for
information concerning your local distributor.

Editorial direction: Ali Gitlow
Copyediting and proofreading: Martha Jay
Design and layout: Paul Sloman/+SUBTRACT
Production: Friederike Schirge
Origination: Repro Ludwig, Zell am See
Printing and binding: Neografia a.s.

Printed in Slovakia
Verlagsgruppe Random House FSC® N001967
The FSC®-certified paper Profisilk has been supplied by Igepa, Germany

ISBN 978-3-7913-4950-3

434482

434482